Hebrew Matters:
110 Hebrew Roots
The Roads They Take
The Stories They Tell

Hebrew Matters:
110 Hebrew Roots
The Roads They Take
The Stories They Tell

Joseph Lowin

AN IMPRINT OF THE
GLOBAL CENTER FOR RELIGIOUS RESEARCH
1312 17TH STREET • SUITE 549
DENVER, COLORADO 80202

INFO@GCRR.ORG • GCRR.ORG

GCRR Press
An imprint of the Global Center for Religious Research
1312 17th Street Suite 549
Denver, CO 80202
www.gcrr.org

Copyright © 2022 by Joseph Lowin

DOI: 10.33929/GCRRPress.2022.02

Typesetter / Copyeditor: Jennifer Walker, Kimberly Dell
Hebraist: Kimberly Dell
Cover Design: Abdullah Al Mahmud
                   fiverr.com/mahmuddidar

Library of Congress Cataloging-in-Publication Data

Hebrew matters: 110 Hebrew roots; the roads they take; the stories they tell / Joseph Lowin
p.   cm.
Includes bibliographic references (p.)
ISBN (Print): 979-8-9857300-4-3
ISBN (eBook): 979-8-9857300-5-0
1. Hebrew language—Textbooks for second language learners—English speakers.   2. Hebrew language—History.   3. Language and culture.
I. Title.

PJ4551.B48   .L695   2022

Remembering Judy

הֲפֹךְ בִּי — אוֹצָר נִמְצָא בִּפְנִים

Search me—a treasure is hidden inside.

What Professionals Have to Say
About the Trilogy

Joseph Lowin's *HebrewSpeak* is essential for anyone wishing to learn the depth and beauty of this ancient tongue that has remained alive and amazingly modern....This brilliant and captivating study of Hebrew roots, reads like a series of tales that will enrich the knowledge of students and teachers alike.

–Elie Wiesel
Nobel Laureate

Dr. Joseph Lowin's *HebrewSpeak* charges us with the magnetism of the Hebrew tongue, turning it like a teacherly kaleidoscope to show us its manifold facets: now wise, humorous, charming; now absorbing, enticing, joyful; and always succinct and surprising. The magical three-letter root, in Dr, Lowin's hands, transforms learning into delight (and vice versa) and pleasure into revelation.

–Cynthia Ozick
Author of *The Puttermesser Papers*

In a very friendly, unconventional, humorous way, *HebrewTalk* conveys to the English-speaking student the beauty of the Hebrew language, demonstrating its etymological sources, its poetic and proverbial facets, its biblical and post-biblical connotations, and its colloquial usages in contemporary spoken Hebrew in Israel. It unites "the pleasant with the useful" for the benefit of all those who wish to learn this old-new language.

–Aharon Megged
Israel Prize Winner,
Member, Israel Hebrew Language Academy

I enjoy … not only the information, but the wit, humor and good sense….From your columns emerges, subtly but powerfully, and without any preachment, the notion that Hebrew is quite the indispensable vehicle for knowing the amalgam of history, religion, culture, experience and wisdom that comprise Judaism.

–Howard Marblestone
Professor of Classical Languages, Lafayette College

Nobody knows the Hebrew language the way Joseph Lowin does. Whether tracing the ethical root of an everyday phrase like "after you," or uncovering the deep-seated connections between Hebrew, Aramaic, and even English, Lowin is a master of Hebrew words, phrases and ideas. To read this book is to journey into history, literature, philosophy and politics. And besides all that, it is wonderful fun, whether you are fluent in Hebrew or just a beginner. So read, learn and talk the talk that Lowin makes so accessible.

–Francine Klagsburn
Author of *Lioness: Golda Meir and the Nation of Israel*

Hebrew language is holy, its very letters sacred. In Joseph Lowin's hands, we see that it is also exuberant, full of rich treasures, fresh as well as ancient, funny as well as profound This is a book for scholars of *leshon ha-kodesh,* for amateur linguists and for ordinary folk who simply like a good read.

–Blu Greenberg
Author of *On Women and Judaism*

What General Readers Have to Say About the Trilogy

This modest-sized book is a treasure trove of insights into the Hebrew language and its unique characteristic of deeper meanings to be found within words. Each page starts with a word and definition; the author then takes you through a fascinating journey of the word's derivation, what it has come to mean, and what Jewish values and teachings it has prompted. I love this book!

It's not a "study book" that is meant to teach Hebrew, but one that meanders through a select list of roots and gives the reader perspective on where the root originated from, how it was used through the ages and how it is used in Modern Hebrew. The author's vast knowledge and research is evident, and the book as a whole is a tribute to the deep history of Hebrew and its amazing evolution to Modern Hebrew. Each root gets about 2 pages of commentary, so it's an easy read and one that doesn't need to be done sequentially. Recommended for anyone who can read Hebrew and has a fundamental comprehension of how words are formed and sentences constructed. It's a fun book for Grammar Geeks and History Buffs alike.

This is a wonderful book to expand your Hebrew knowledge. The stories that go along with each root tell so much about the Jewish value system. Thank you for sharing this wonderful information.

If you are new to learning Hebrew, this book will surely wind up in your book collection. This book brings Hebrew words to life through etymology.

Contents

Preface

*From the Dust of the Earth
to the Repair of the World*

In a short story that appeared first in *The New Yorker*, Cynthia Ozick, herself an American master of English prose, reveals a predilection for the Hebrew language. Her fondness for Hebrew stems from a profound understanding of the mechanisms by which Hebrew operates. Introducing the heroine of the novel that derived from that story, *The Puttermesser Papers* (Knopf, 1997), Ozick dilates on Ruth Puttermesser's fascination with Hebrew grammar and the allure of the three-letter root on which its vocabulary is based. Ozick writes: "The permutations of the triple-lettered root elated her; how was it possible that a whole language, hence a whole literature, a civilization even, should rest on the pure presence of three letters of the alphabet? ... It seemed to her not so much a language for expression as a code for the world's design... The idea of the grammar of Hebrew turned Puttermesser's brain into a sort of palace, a sort of Vatican; inside its corridors she walked from one resplendent triptych to another."

For more than thirty years I have been walking along the corridors of these same Vaticans and palaces. Moreover, as the Hebrew Language columnist at Hadassah Magazine during this time, I have had the pleasure of elucidating for thousands of readers not only the mechanisms of the triliteral (three-letter) root of Hebrew, but also the beauty of Hebrew vocabulary as it develops in Biblical, Talmudic, Medieval, and Modern Hebrew, right up through the colorful slang of the streets and fields of the modern State of Israel. This has been accomplished not only in the Magazine but in two previous books—*Hebrew Speak* and *Hebrew Talk*—based on these columns. Since their publication, these two books have attracted thousands of readers. For this new book, *Hebrew*

Matters, I have compiled one hundred and ten columns written for Hadassah Magazine in recent years.

Over the years, I have considered each column I write an ode to the Hebrew language. Often, the poetry metaphor takes my mind a little too far. While I am editing a draft of a column for Hadassah Magazine, I will start thinking that the 450-word limit the magazine imposes is like the 14-line restriction on the sonnets of Shakespeare and Petrarch I had studied as a young man. I then proceed from there to the comparison of my three volumes of musings on more than 300 Hebrew roots to Petrarch's *Canzoniere* of 300 and more sonnets. Eventually, returning to earth, I mumble to myself, "Get off your high horse, Dr. Joe!"; and then I go back, a bit more modestly, to the root in question.

Each root is presented with a light touch and spiced with a good measure of humor. As one reader wrote, on the Amazon web site, "This [book] makes Hebrew vocabulary easy to learn and remember. . . .But it's also fun, because there is plenty of cleverness, wit, and cultural flavor to the twists and meanings flowing through the connections. And this book is about the fun, funny, sarcastic, and joyful bits of the language. Far from being a dry, analytical work, it's full of stories, quips, jokes, and overall love and reverence for Hebrew."

In this book I try to capture how the Hebrew language "matters" to us today. What I am interested in learning is how Hebrew makes its way through the roads and byways it takes and how the stories it tells through its three-letter roots travel to the various worlds that make up Jewish civilization through the ages. Almost every word spoken in the places where Hebrew has flourished resonates with the echoes of Jewish history, Jewish civilization, and the Jewish textual tradition. Readers of this book are invited to listen in to the stories of Hebrew told here in the hope that these echoes will resonate with them as well.

Riverdale, New York
December 21, 2021

A Note on Translation and Transliteration

The three-letter roots that form the basis of this book are presented in Hebrew characters in the title of each chapter, in Hebrew alphabetical order, *alef* to *tav*—from the dust of the earth in chapter 1, to the repair of the world in chapter 110. Words derived from each root are then presented in the body of each chapter, in Hebrew, together with the vowel points—dots and dashes—that make it easier for readers to read. The Hebrew of these words and phrases is followed by a transliteration into English letters, to help readers familiarize themselves with the sounds of Hebrew. Finally, all the Hebrew words are translated into English. This is all done in what I hope is companionable prose designed to capture the reader's interest. Because this book is intended for pleasurable reading, as though it were a conversation with our readers and not a vocabulary list, not all our translations are literal or exact. For example, in many cases we have tried to find equivalents of Israeli slang in American idioms. In a great many other cases, for the sake of accessibility, we have aimed to "converse" rather than translate the Hebrew into English, in what one might call a *converslation*, so that even the translation tells a story that engages the reader.

As to the transliterations, *Hebrew Matters* generally follows the transliteration rules of the *Encyclopedia Judaica* (Jerusalem: Keter, 1972), Vol. 1, p. 90. In addition, because even transliteration is not immune to trends, fashions, and elaborations, I have from time to time deviated from the rules when it has appeared prudent to do so for the sake of our readers' comfort. Many Hebrew words have entered the English language and have found a home there, in dictionaries, the street, and advertisements. In the body of this text, that's how they may appear as well. When they are transliterations of the Hebrew, however, the spelling will follow our rules of transliteration. Take the example of unleavened bread. In English, it may be "Matzoh"; in the transliteration, (*matsah*).

Acknowledgements

After many other occasions to do so during our long life together, cut short by the Coronavirus pandemic, I am once again pleased to thank my late wife, Judith, the first reader of everything I had written for publication. Her sharp eye went beyond hunting for typographical errors. She was also expert at detecting and repairing all types of pedantry, sophistry, and overly technical language. For coming to my technological rescue at the many times it was needed—and especially when it was getting close to the wire—I am indebted to our children, Shari, David and Benji.

In addition, I would like to thank Alan Tigay, the executive editor at Hadassah Magazine at the time, for inviting me in the first place to write the columns that make up the content of what are now three volumes about Hebrew roots and their derivations, and Lisa Hostein, the magazine's current executive editor, who took the initiative to return my column to its place in the Hadassah firmament after a brief hiatus. This is also the place to praise the Hadassah organization itself for its steadfast commitment over the years to The Jerusalem Program, in which a central plank is Hebrew education and the teaching of Hebrew as the national language of the Jewish people.

My most faithful companions over the years have been the Hebrew lexicographers and scholars whose weighty dictionaries landed with a pleasant thud on my dining room table each month, as I was beginning a new chapter in my way of telling the Hebrew story. It is a pleasure to list their names here: Reuven Alkalai; Avraham Even-Shoshan; Yaacov Choueka; Eitan Avneyon; Abraham Solomonick; Ruth Almagor-Ramon; Ruvik Rosenthal; Dan Ben-Amotz, Netiva Ben-Yehuda; and Avshalom Kor. Truly, any such list begins and ends with Eliezer Ben Yehuda, whose dictionary I paged through not in my dining room but in the stacks of Columbia University's Butler Library in New York. Lost in the heady odors emanating from those old volumes, as I moved from a new linguistic discovery to a new Judaica insight, I often dreamt of Ben Yehuda as the best Jew of my lifetime, even though he had died 20 years before my birth.

I owe a great debt as well to Roselyn Bell, Zelda Shluker, and most recently Leah Finkelshteyn, my editors at Hadassah Magazine over the years, for their tender loving care of the columns that arrived on their desks at regular intervals, for enhancing my prose, making it readable for the general audiences for which it was intended and, when it was called for, for making sure that any inaccuracies that had crept in would be duly corrected.

Furthermore, I am grateful to Walter Herzberg, a good friend with whom I had been reunited after many years during which we had lost touch with each other, for sharing his vast knowledge and love of Hebrew grammar, philology and usage. Rabbi Joseph Brodie has been an invaluable Judaica resource who, like Chaucer's cleric, would "gladly learn and gladly teach," and would do so with exemplary patience. I am grateful to Erica Goldman-Brodie, a master of the WorldWideWeb who, together with her own worldwide web of contacts, would uncannily find what I needed when I needed it. I am greatly beholden to my learned daughter-in-law Avital Malina for reading the proofs of this book before it went to press and for making sure that it is as close as humanly possible to being error-free. It goes without saying that I am nevertheless solely answerable for any errors that remain.

I would like to thank Darren Slade, President of the Global Center for Religious Research, and Publisher as well of its GCRR Press, for his instant and enduring enthusiasm for this project. I am especially thankful to Jennifer Walker and Kimberly Dell, of the editorial staff at GCRR Press, for their keen discernment and judicious comments, suggestions and corrections.

Finally, it is difficult to assess the many ways in which Richard White, a good friend of many years, shared his skills in the use of proper English, his deep knowledge of Semitic languages and his expertise in information technology. I have over the course of these many years considered him my teacher in a broad range of subjects relating to the humanities. More than any other, after uncountable telephone conversations and shared text messages and e-mails, he has been instrumental in helping me turn my manuscript into a book.

Wrestling with Dust

א-ב-ק

alef-vet-kof

Theart educators at the J. Paul Getty Museum in Los Angeles
teach that to gain insight into a work of art, you have to train
yourself to "look longer." Similarly, look hard and long
enough at a Hebrew root and you will find an abundance of insight
into the art of Jewish living. For example, look at the root א-ב-ק (*alef,
vet, kof*) and you will uncover: dust and wrestling, perfume and
pollen, a certain male organ and slander, buttonholes, a lung
ailment—and grandma's vacuum cleaner.

According to Hebrew etymologist Ernest Klein, the word
אָבָק (*avak*), dust, is related to an Arabic word meaning that which
flies or flees. Throw soot toward the sky, as Moses does in Exodus,
and noxious *avak* will fly out all over the land of Egypt. The
marketplace enters into the lyricism of the *Song of Songs* with our
root, as the beloved arrives, enveloped in clouds of perfume made
from אַבְקַת רוֹכֵל (*avkat rokhel*), literally, merchant's powder.

Rashi disagrees with medieval philologist Menahem ben
Saruk about the narrative of Jacob's wrestling match with an angel.
For ben Saruk, the phrase וַיֵּאָבֵק אִישׁ עִמּוֹ (*va-ye'avek ish immo*)
signifies that Jacob and the "man" raised dust while wrestling. For
Rashi, however, *avak* is related to חֲבַק (*havak*), Aramaic for he
fastened himself on, or intertwined himself. Think of the way a
twined אֶבֶק (*evek*), loop, is made. *Pirke Avot* uses both embracing
and dust metaphorically, telling us, הֱוֵי מִתְאַבֵּק בַּעֲפַר רַגְלֵיהֶם (*hevei
mitabbek ba-afar ragleihem*), "Cling to the dust of their feet," i.e.,
study at the feet of the sages. The rabbis take this dust even more
abstractly, taking the word *avak* to mean a hint of, or smidgen. Thus,
Maimonides forbids not only slander, but even "a hint of slander,"
אֲבַק לְשׁוֹן הָרָע (*avak leshon ha-ra*). Thus, Maimonides forbids one to

even speak *well* of a person in front of his enemy, lest the latter take this as an opening to speak *ill* of him.

Today, too much dust in the air can lead to אַבֶּקֶת (*abbeket*), coniosis, a disease of the lungs. While הָאֲבָקָה (*ha'avakah*), crop dusting, is used by farmers to kill harmful insects, the אַבְקָן (*avkan*), male sexual organ of the flower—stamen—is used by nature to perform אֲבָקָה (*avakah*), pollination. Israeli novelist Meir Shalev, in a memoir of his childhood in Nahalal, tells a charming story of his Russian grandmother and her American שׁוֹאֵב אָבָק (*sho'ev avak*), vacuum cleaner.

This has not been too much of a מַאֲבָק (*ma'avak*), struggle. To gain insight from a Hebrew root, you need only look longer and deeper.

Learning of Love

א-ה-ב

alef-heh-vet

If he hadn't been told of love, he would never have considered loving," observed French philosopher Blaise Pascal. Whether love does come naturally or is an acquired trait, the Torah uses the root א-ה-ב (*alef, heh, vet*), love, to command the love of both God and humankind. On the one hand we are instructed וְאָהַבְתָּ אֵת ה' אֱלוֹקֶיךָ (*ve-ahavta et hashem elokekha*), "Love the Lord, your God," and on the other וְאָהַבְתָּ לְרֵעֲךָ כָּמוֹךָ (*ve-ahavta le-rei'akha kamokha*), "Love your neighbor as yourself."

The Bible is generously seasoned with words of love that sometimes lead to dramatic scenes. Abraham is told to take the son אֲשֶׁר אָהַבְתָּ (*asher ahavta*), "whom you love," Isaac, and sacrifice him. Joseph's sojourn in Egypt comes about because וְיִשְׂרָאֵל אָהַב אֶת יוֹסֵף (*ve-yisra'el ahav et yosef*), "Jacob loved Joseph," more than his other sons. Proverbs warns its young acolyte melodramatically to beware of the woman who entices him with the phrase נִתְעַלְּסָה בָּאֳהָבִים (*nitalsa ba-ahavim*), "Let us couple in amorous embrace."

Biblical love is nevertheless often spiritual, especially in the story of Jonathan and David, whose relationship, David insists, surpasses אַהֲבַת נָשִׁים (*ahavat nashim*), the love of women. The Psalmist chants of his love of God, while *Song of Songs* sings another tune, as the beloved speaks of being חוֹלַת אַהֲבָה (*holat ahava*), lovesick.

The rabbis explain the suffering of the righteous with a concept called יִסוּרִים שֶׁל אַהֲבָה (*yisurim shel ahava*), afflictions of love, i.e., suffering in this world to suffer less in the world to come. They also recognize God's love for humanity in אַהֲבָה רַבָּה (*ahava rabba*), great love.

The title of A.B. Yehoshua's first novel is הַמְאַהֵב (*ha-me'ahev*), *The Lover*, and אַהֲבָה (*ahava*) is a four-letter square sculpture by Robert Indiana at the Israel Museum. Eliezer Ben-Yehuda got into the act when he coined the word אֲהַבְהָבִים (*ahavhavim*), flirting, based on our root. Ruth Almagor Ramon, author of *Rega Shel Ivrit* on Hebrew usage, uses our root to teach a lesson in studied ambiguity. The two-noun construction אַהֲבַת הוֹרִים (*ahavat horim*) can be either parent's love for children or children's love for parents. Using our root and the same two-noun construction, Ramon comes up with an adjectival phrase, אַהֲבַת נֶפֶשׁ (*ahavat nefesh*), profound love.

The question remains: Is love a learned condition? To some, אַהֲבַת הַבְּרִיּוֹת (*ahavat ha-beriyot*), love of humankind, does come naturally. To others, learning the Hebrew word for love is sufficient.

Shewayah Shewayah

א-ט-ט
alef-tet-tet

Despite the ever-increasing demand these days for "fast, faster and fastest," there are still a few relaxed folks who like to take their time. If you can't imagine where these people might be found, take a tour of the Mediterranean basin, where you will hear: Italian *piano piano;* Greek *siga siga;* Turkish *yavash yavash;* Arabic *shewayeh shewayeh;* and one of many Hebrew idioms for "take it easy," לְאַט לְאַט (*le'at le'at*), slowly slowly.

Some linguists conjecture that the root from which *le'at* derives, א-ט-ט (*alef, tet, tet*), was used by Isaiah in the word אִטִּים (*ittim*), referring to sorcerers who would mutter soft, slow and moaning sounds. Isaiah also records that the waters of Shiloah הֹלְכִים לְאַט (*holkhim le'at*), "flow gently." When Elijah rebukes King Ahab for his crimes, the sinner demonstrates his repentance by becoming אַט (*at*), "subdued." One of the "comforters" of Job rebukes him with the question וְדָבָר לָאַט עִמְּךָ? (*ve-davar la'at immakh*), "Are you privy to [cosmic] secrets?" Possibly the most touching use of the root in Scripture is ascribed to King David. Fearful of the fate of his rebellious son Absalom, David pleads, לְאַט לִי לַנַּעַר (*le'at li la-na'ar*), "For my sake deal gently with the lad." In a decidedly ungentle episode in the Book of Judges, Yael approaches the enemy warrior Sisera בַּלָּאט (*ba-la'at*), "in secret," the more efficiently to slay him.

The poet Hayyim Nahman Bialik plays musically on the similarity of sound between עֵת (*et*), time, and אַט (*et*), slow, saying, הַהוֹלֵךְ לְאִטּוֹ יָבוֹא בְּעִתּוֹ (*ha-holekh le-itto yavo be-itto*), "He who goes slowly comes on time." We can all agree that at times טַחֲנוֹת הַצֶּדֶק טוֹחֲנוֹת לְאַט (*tahanot ha-tsedek tohanot le'at*), "The mills of justice grind slowly." In Israel today you may hold up your hand, palm out, and say לְאַט לְךָ! (*le'at lekha*), "Take it easy!" Arik Einstein's popular song סַע לְאַט (*sa le'at*), "Drive Slowly," was adapted by Israel's Pizza Hut as an advertising slogan, סַע לְהָאט (*sa la-hat*), Drive to the Hut. Avraham Hefner's groundbreaking 1967 short film לְאַט יוֹתֵר (*le'at yoter*), *Slow Down!*, was adapted from a story by Simone de Beauvoir.

Driving in Israel, you'll probably encounter our root on road signs warning, הָאֵט! מַחְסוֹם לְפָנֶיךָ (*ha'et mahsom lefanekha*), Slow Down! Barrier Ahead. A sign in a residential neighborhood may inform you of the פַּסֵּי הָאֲטָה (*passei he'atah*), Speed Bumps. Then there is the dietary ditty: אֱכוֹל מְעַט, אֱכוֹל לְאַט (*ekhol me'at ekhol le'at*), Eat little, eat slowly. Of course, for those who require a break from their fast-paced lives, a most congenial suggestion might be לְאַט אֲבָל בָּטוּחַ (*le'at aval batu'ah*), slowly but surely.

How'm I doing?

א-י-כ

alef-yod-khof

It is widely held that הָאֵיכוּת חֲשׁוּבָה מֵהַכַּמּוּת (*ha-eikhut hashuva me-ha-kammut*), quality is more important than quantity. The words אֵיכוּת (*eikhut*), quality, and כַּמּוּת (*kammut*), quantity—found in neither biblical nor talmudic literature but present throughout medieval Hebrew texts—are coined from אֵיךְ (*eikh*), how, and כַּמָּה (*kamma*), how much. Strikingly, each word encompasses both quality and quantity and is therefore important enough to merit individual treatment.

The root א-י-כ (*alef, yod, khof*) has a verb form, לְאַיֵּךְ (*le-ayyekh*), to qualify, that is rarely used. In Scripture, the root mainly appears in rhetorical questions and exclamations of grief or astonishment. In Genesis, King Abimelekh scolds Isaac for lying to him, asking, אֵיךְ אָמַרְתָּ (*eikh amarta*), "How could you say" Rebekah was your sister? Later, Judah begs to be substituted for Benjamin as hostage, arguing אֵיךְ אֶעֱלֶה (*eikh e'eleh*), "How can I go back up" to my father without the boy? In David's elegy commemorating the deaths of Saul and Jonathan, we find the quintessential expression of despair, אֵיךְ נָפְלוּ גִבּוֹרִים (*eikh naflu gibborim*), "How the mighty have fallen!"

Grief is deepened as the *eikh* is drawn out. On Tisha B'Av, we memorialize the destruction of the Temple by chanting the Book of Lamentations: אֵיכָה יָשְׁבָה בָדָד (*eikha yashva vadad*), "How does [the city that was full of people] sit so desolate?" Esther adds another syllable and further poetic poignancy, justifying her request to King Ahasuerus that he rescind Haman's evil decree, pleading אֵיכָכָה אוּכַל וְרָאִיתִי (*eikhakha ukhal ve-ra'iti*), "How can I bear to see" evil done to my people?

Today, we are interested in אֵיכוּתִי (*eikhuti*), qualitative issues like אֵיכוּת הַסְּבִיבָה (*eikhut ha-seviva*), quality of the environment, and

אֵיכוּת הַחַיִּים (*eikhut ha-hayyim*), quality of life. Modern Hebrew also uses the root in many popular expressions, from אֵיךְ קוֹרְאִים לְךָ (*eikh kor'im lekha*), what do they call you?, to אֵיךְ הָעִנְיָנִים (*eikh ha-inyanim*), how're things? One might argue, אֵיכְשֶׁהוּ (*eikhshehu*), somehow, and אֵיךְ שֶׁלֹּא יִהְיֶה (*eikh she-lo yiheyeh*), no matter what, that its widest use is in the exclamation וְעוֹד אֵיךְ (*ve-od eikh*), you better believe it!

Crooning in Hebrew slang a chanson by Georges Brassens, Israeli folksinger Yossi Banai asks a recently deceased friend, presumably in heaven, to inquire of Mother Eve, אֵיךְ הַמַּרְגָּשׁ (*eikh ha-margash*), "How're you feeling?" So, does quantity generate quality? We'll explore that issue in Chapter 42, with כַּמָּה מִלִּים (*kamma milim*), a few well-chosen words.

A Man and a Woman?

א-י-ש

alef-yod-shin

The question of the origins of men and women has received much attention, with advocates adducing biblical, scientific and sociopolitical explanations for the genesis of humankind. No less interesting than this hot topic is the debate around the origins of the Hebrew words אִישׁ (*ish*), man, and אִשָּׁה (*isha*), woman.

The 19th-century German rabbi, Samson Raphael Hirsch, suggests that the verbal root א-י-שׁ (*alef, yod, shin*) is related to יֵשׁ (*yesh*), there is, meaning "to exist." The *Brown-Driver-Briggs Hebrew and English Lexicon* (Oxford University Press) speaks of "the impossibility of deriving אִישׁ and אִשָּׁה from the same root, "since the *dagesh* in the *shin* in אִשָּׁה hints at a missing letter. The *BDB* entertains the notion of a root א-נ-שׁ (*alef, nun, shin*), which would give us not only אִשָּׁה, but also אֱנוֹשׁ (*enosh*), humankind; הָאֲנָשָׁה (*ha'anasha*), personification; and the plurals אֲנָשִׁים (*anashim*), men, and נָשִׁים (*nashim*), women. However, the *BDB* concludes, "probability seems to favor the root א-י-שׁ."

The Bible has no difficulty seeing *ish* and *isha* as masculine and feminine forms of the same word. Adam, who names all living things, declares לְזֹאת יִקָּרֵא אִשָּׁה כִּי מֵאִישׁ לֻקֳחָה (*le-zot yikkare isha ki me-ish lukaha*), "She shall be called woman because she was taken from man." The pairs of animals led into Noah's Ark are called אִישׁ וְאִשְׁתּוֹ (*ish ve-ishto*), male and female.

Jacob is אִישׁ תָּם (*ish tam*), a simple man, and Esau אִישׁ יֹדֵעַ צַיִד (*ish yode'a tsayid*), a cunning hunter. Since the prophetess Deborah is אֵשֶׁת לַפִּידוֹת (*eshet lappidot*), the wife of Lapidot, the term today is applied to a strong, energetic woman. King David may not build the Temple because he is אִישׁ מִלְחָמוֹת (*ish milhamot*), a man of wars, while God Himself is praised as אִישׁ מִלְחָמָה (*ish milhama*), Man of War. The Talmud's taboo against using the name of Jesus gives us אוֹתוֹ הָאִישׁ (*oto ha-ish*), That Man. *Pirkei Avot* traces history from Moses—whom the Torah dubs הָאִישׁ (*ha-ish*), the man—to אַנְשֵׁי כְּנֶסֶת הַגְּדוֹלָה (*anshei kenesset ha-gedola*), the Men of the Great Assembly.

Today, we speak of the common man as הָאִישׁ בָּרְחוֹב (*ha-ish ba-rehov*), the man in the street, or אַנְשֵׁי הַשּׁוּרָה (*anshei ha-shura*), the rank and file. One might refer אִישִׁית (*ishit*), personally, to a public אִישִׁיּוּת (*ishi'ut*), personality, as an אִישׁ אֶשְׁכּוֹלוֹת (*ish eshkolot*), Renaissance man, one whose name is found in סֵפֶר הָאִישִׁים (*sefer ha-ishim*), *Who's Who*. In דִינֵי אִישׁוּת (*dinei ishut*), the laws of matrimony, אִשְׁתּוֹ כְּגוּפוֹ (*ishto ke-gufo*), a man's wife is considered to be like the man himself. Original, isn't it?

You Don't Say

א-מ-ר
alef-mem-resh

"I t isn't what it's talking about that makes a book Jewish—it's that
the book won't shut up." So said Philip Roth, author of several
books in which Jews can't stop talking. But is he aware that the
simple Hebrew root א-מ-ר (*alef, mem, resh*), to say, reveals as much
about Jewish mores as his droll אִמְרָה (*imra*), aphorism? Variations
on the formula "God spoke to Moses, לֵאמֹר (*leimor*), saying," appear
more than 900 times in Scripture. The root is also found in some
potentially violent biblical narratives. For example, Rebekah sends
her son Jacob into exile when she learns—how, we do not know—
that his twin brother, Esau, אָמַר בְּלִבּוֹ (*amar be-libbo*), "was plotting
in his heart," to kill him. The root also introduces the exile of Moses
to Midian, where he flees after hearing the veiled threat הַלְהָרְגֵנִי אַתָּה
אֹמֵר (*ha-le-horgeini ata omer*), "Do you mean to kill me" as you
killed the Egyptian overseer? More sentimentally, in Egypt, Joseph
asks his brothers if their father אֲשֶׁר אֲמַרְתֶּם (*asher amartem*), "whom
you mentioned," is well.

When one combines the "titles" of three consecutive weekly
readings in *Leviticus—aharei mot,* after death; *kedoshim,* holy; and
אֱמֹר (*emor*), say—one may come up with the advice, "Say only
positive things of the dead." Possibly the cleverest use of our root is
found in an article by modern Hebrew-language maven Ben-Zion
Fischler: אִמְרֵי חֲזַ"ל שֶׁחֲזַ"ל לֹא אֲמָרוּם (*imrei hazal she-hazal lo
amarum*), "Sayings of the Rabbis That the Rabbis Never Said."

The rabbis did say many things, of course, calling a whole
class of its sages אָמוֹרָאִים (*amoraim*), speakers. When some rabbis
would come upon a difficult biblical verse, they might declare, זֶה
אוֹמֵר דּוֹרְשֵׁנִי (*zeh omer dorsheni*), this verse calls for a midrashic
interpretation. In a dispute, one might find the expression יֵשׁ אוֹמְרִים
(*yesh omerim*), there are those of a different opinion.

One way to bring redemption to the world in the Jewish value system is to cite a quotation בְּשֵׁם אוֹמְרוֹ (*be-shem omero*), in the name of its originator, זֹאת אוֹמֶרֶת (*zot omeret*), that means, give credit for an idea that is not yours. The root is widespread in colloquial Hebrew, where the literal meaning might take on slangy overtones. Thus, you might hear expressions such as מָה אַתָּה אוֹמֵר (*mah atta omer*), You must be kidding! Or זֶה לֹא אוֹמֵר לִי כְּלוּם (*zeh lo omer li kelum*), I don't care for this at all.

Or you might just read a מַאֲמָר (*ma'amar*), article, that reminds you not of Philip Roth but of a מֵימְרָה (*meimra*), saying, from *Pirke Avot:* אֱמֹר מְעַט (*emor me'at*), Say little, but do a lot.

Plenty of Nothin'

א-פ-ס

alef-feh-samekh

Who would want to take credit for inventing nothing? That is perhaps why it is difficult to trace the history of the number zero. Was it the Babylonians? The Mayans? The Indians? The Arabs? The latter are indeed credited with having introduced zero to the West, via a word related to the Hebrew *sefira,* number. Nevertheless, another root, א-פ-ס (*alef, feh, samekh*), originally meaning extremity, is the Hebrew equivalent for zero.

Genesis tells us that during the famine in Egypt, the people came to Joseph, Pharaoh's vizier, to beg for bread, כִּי אָפֵס כָּסֶף (*ki afes kassef*), "because [our] money has run out." Isaiah berates the Babylonians for falsely thinking to themselves אֲנִי וְאַפְסִי עוֹד (*ani ve-afsi od*), "I am, and none else is besides me." He reminds Persia's King Cyrus, on behalf of God, אֶפֶס בִּלְעָדָי (*efes bil'adai*), "There is none but Me." Isaiah also quotes the nations of the world, who will one day declare אֵין עוֹד אֶפֶס (*ein od efes*), "there is no other," but God. In Numbers, the 12 scouts add a caveat to their praise of Canaan: אֶפֶס כִּי עַז הָעָם (*efes ki az ha-am*), "however, the nation [dwelling there] is strong."

The expression אַפְסֵי אָרֶץ (*afsei arets*), the ends of the earth, is found a dozen times in Scripture in its original sense, extremity. Using our root metaphorically to make an ethical point, Proverbs remarks בְּאֶפֶס עֵצִים (*be-efes etsim*), "absent trees" (i.e., talebearers), the fires of strife go out. Ezekiel's expression מֵי אָפְסָיִם (*mei ofsayim*), water that reaches the ankles, is used today to mean shallow water. Medieval grammarian Jonah Ibn Janakh suggests that shallow water does not come from *efes,* but rather from פַּס (*pas*), sole of the foot, making *mei ofsayim* both shallower and more logical.

Today, the verb אִפֵּס (*ifes*), to annihilate, is also used in the Army to "zero" an instrument. A physicist may lecture to a hall filled

עַד אֶפֶס מָקוֹם (*ad efes makom*), to capacity, about אֶפֶס מֻחְלָט (*efes muhlat*), absolute zero. Some people are lucky enough to get things done בְּאֶפֶס יָד (*be-efes yad*), without trying too hard, or even בְּאֶפֶס מַעֲשֶׂה (*be-efes ma'aseh*), without doing anything at all. While some people are philosophical אֶפְסָנִים (*afsanim*), nihilists, there are several ways using slang to characterize a person who is an אֶפֶס גָּמוּר (*efes gamur*), real big nothing. Compare an אֶפֶס בַּר אֶפֶס (*efes bar efes*), zero, son of zero; אֶפֶס אֲפָסִים (*efes afasim*), a zero to end all zeroes; אֶפֶס בְּרִבּוּעַ (*efes be-ribu'a*), a zero squared; and אֶפֶס מְאוּפָּס (*efes me-ufas*), a zeroed zero. Who would have thought that in a land flowing with milk and honey there could be such a plethora of zeroes?

On the Other Road

א-ר-ח

alef-resh-het

W hen an Israeli travels abroad today, he carries a דַּרְכּוֹן (*darkon*), passport, from the word דֶּרֶךְ (*derekh*), road. A century ago, one's passport might have been called an אָרְחִית (*orhit*)—a word that has fallen entirely into disuse—from a parallel ancient Hebrew root that has survived and sometimes flourished, א-ר-ח (*alef, resh, het*), to travel.

In Scripture, this root is found in connection with two important narratives. In the Joseph story, when the youngster, doted upon by his father, is thrown into a pit by his envious brothers, his life is saved thanks to a passing אֹרְחַת יִשְׁמְעֵאלִים (*orhat yishme'elim*), "caravan of Ishmaelites." When foremother Sarah, in old age, is told that she is to bear a child, she is incredulous. After all, she has ceased to exhibit אֹרַח כַּנָּשִׁים (*orah ka-nashim*), "the 'way' of women," a euphemism for the menses that indicate fertility. The psalmist finds this figurative sense of the root particularly useful, especially when he entreats, לַמְּדֵנִי אֹרְחֹתֶיךָ (*orhoteha lamdeini*), "Teach me Thy ways."

The rabbis of the Talmud used an Aramaic term containing our root to speak of something incidental to a main argument, אַגַּב אוֹרְחָא (*agav orha*), "by the way." In deciding Jewish law, the Talmud, foregoing strict legalism, stakes out a claim for local custom, אוֹרַח אַרְעָא (*orah ar'ah*), the "way of the land."

Modern Hebrew writers often demonstrate a classical flair by using Aramaic idioms. Bringing into play our root, Hayyim Nahman Bialik chastises אָרְחֵי פָּרְחֵי (*orhei porhei*), vagrants; S.Y. Agnon relates that one politely asks a wayfarer where he is from, כְּאוֹרַח גּוּבְרִין יְהוּדָאִין (*ke-orah guvrin yehuda'in*), "after the manner of Jewish gentlemen."

The root has taken on usages that have mainly to do with hospitality, especially in the words אוֹרֵחַ (*ore'ah*), guest, and אֲרוּחָה (*aruhah*), meal. A luxury hotel in Tel Aviv advertises that it practices אֲרוּחַ כְּיַד הַמֶּלֶךְ (*eru'ah ke-yad ha-melekh*), hospitality fit for a king. Visitors, having tasted Israeli hotels' sumptuous אֲרוּחַת בּוֹקֶר (*aruhat boker*), breakfast, might be willing to forego the locals' אֲרוּחַת עֶשֶׂר (*aruhat esser*), 10 A.M. snack; אֲרוּחַת צָהֳרַים (*aruhat tsohorayim*), lunch; and אֲרוּחַת אַרְבַּע (*aruhat arba*), 4 P.M. snack. By the time of אֲרוּחַת עֶרֶב (*aruhat erev*), dinner, however, they may appreciate being אוֹרְחִים (*orhim*), guests, at an אֲרוּחַת שְׁחִיתוּת (*aruhat shehitut*), copious meal of many courses.

Dieters may prefer an אֲרוּחַת יָרָק (*aruhat yarak*), light meal of greens. But next time you go לְהִתְאָרֵחַ (*le-hitare'ah*), to be a guest, at the home of an Israeli family, bring to your מְאָרְחִים (*me-arhim*), hosts, both a hearty appetite and a nice box of Israeli chocolates.

9

Coming, Going—And Then Some

ב-ו-א

bet-vav-alef

Have you ever felt you didn't know whether you were coming or going? Well, Hebrew has a root that might feel that way. Depending on context, ב-ו-א (*bet, vav, alef*) means to come, to go—and many more surprising things as well. It makes sense that a root found some 3,000 times in Scripture would have a wide variety of meanings. In Genesis, Abraham is בָּא בַּיָּמִים (*ba ba-yamim*), old. A barren Rachel offers Jacob her servant Bilha and says, בֹּא אֵלֶיהָ (*bo eileha*), "Lie with her." Reuben, learning of his brother Joseph's disappearance, laments אָנָה אֲנִי בָא (*ana ani ba*), "Where shall I turn ?" In Exodus, God instructs Moses בֹּא אֶל פַּרְעֹה (*bo el par'oh*), "Go to Pharaoh." Leviticus decrees וּבָא הַשֶּׁמֶשׁ וְטָהֵר (*u-va ha-shemesh ve-taher*), "When the sun sets [the Priest] is cleansed." In Numbers, Moses confronts the tribes who want to settle in Transjordan with, "Your brothers יָבֹאוּ לַמִּלְחָמָה (*yavo'u la-milhama*), will go to war, and you'll stay here?"

To intensify a Hebrew verb one doubles it. In *Tanakh*, בֹּא יָבֹא (*bo yavo*) means both "He will certainly come" and "It always comes true." The Bible also uses the root to point out a route, e.g., בֹּאֲךָ גְרָרָה (*bo'akha gerara*), "as you come toward Gerar." Look closely and you'll recognize our root in תְּבוּאָה (*tevu'a*), crop, the produce coming to us from the land.

The Sages of the Talmud used our root לְהָבִיא רְאָיָה (*le-havi re-aya*), to bring a proof, and to declare that בִּיאָה (*bi'a*), cohabitation, is one way of consecrating a marriage. In the Shabbat liturgy, we greet the Sabbath angels with בּוֹאֲכֶם לְשָׁלוֹם (*bo'akhem le-shalom*), come in peace. Then there is the mystical עוֹלָם הַבָּא (*olam ha-ba*), world to come.

In modern Israel, you're likely to hear opening gambits like לְהַבָּא (*le-ha-ba*), from now on; בֹּא נַגִּיד (*bo naggid*), let us say; and

בָּרוּךְ הַבָּא (*barukh ha-ba*), welcome. A proposal may be rejected out of hand with a gruff לֹא בָּא בְּחֶשְׁבּוֹן (*lo ba be-heshbon*), out of the question! A מָבוֹא (*mavo*) is a preface, leading the reader into a book.

Songwriter Ehud Manor, using our root twice, celebrates those who come on *aliya* in the refrain בָּא לִי לְהַגִּיד כַּמָּה טוֹב שֶׁבָּאתֶם (*ba li le-haggid kamma tov she-batem*), "I really want to say 'I'm very glad you came.'" Less sentimentally, that welcoming plaque inscribed בָּרוּךְ אַתָּה בְּבוֹאֶךָ (*barukh ata be-vo'ekha*), "Bless you as you come in," has been seen bearing a scribbled addendum reading, "All the more so as you go out."

Maybe it's time for us to go as well.

10

Nine-tenths of the Law

ב-ע-ל
bet-ayin-lamed

How does one take possession? Hebrew offers an understanding of the issue of בַּעֲלוּת (*ba'alut*), ownership, through the root ב-ע-ל (*bet, ayin, lamed*), to own, rule over, marry, have sexual relations. Early on, the noun, בַּעַל (*ba'al*), owner, was the name of the powerful Canaanite god, Ba'al, worshiped as owner of the land who provided rainfall to make the soil fertile. The verb בָּעַל (*ba'al*) meant to take possession of a territory by entering and fructifying it. It is not difficult to see how the root came to be used in connection with marriage and בְּעִילָה (*be'ila*), sexual congress.

In the Book of Esther, the Persian king's advisers argue that rebellious Queen Vashti should be deposed so that wives in his realm יִתְּנוּ יְקָר לְבַעְלֵיהֶן (*yitnu yekar le-va'aleihen*), "show respect to their husbands." The prophet Isaiah reminds Israel that even an ass knows how to find אֵבוּס בְּעָלָיו (*evus be'alav*), "the feeding trough of its owner." The same Isaiah renames the land of Israel בְּעוּלָה (*be'ula*), espoused, presumably to God. (The woman's name Beulah surely comes from this source.) Joseph is called derisively by his brothers בַּעַל הַחֲלוֹמוֹת (*ba'al ha-halomot*), "the dream man," where *ba'al* refers not to ownership but to his possession of a singular trait.

In both classical and modern Hebrew, *ba'al* is used in dozens of compound expressions. The founder of the Hasidic movement was known as the בַּעַל שֵׁם טוֹב (*ba'al shem tov*), Master of the Good Name. In the synagogue, we have a בַּעַל תְּפִילָה (*ba'al tefilla*), prayer leader, to say nothing of the בַּעַל תְּשׁוּבָה (*ba'al teshuva*), penitent. One way of referring to the Jewish God is בַּעַל הָרַחֲמִים (*ba'al ha-rahamim*), the Merciful One.

A בַּעַל חַיִּים (*ba'al hayyim*) suggests anything endowed with life. Today, however, the term is applied almost exclusively to animals, as in Israel's חֶבְרַת צַעַר בַּעֲלֵי חַיִּים (*hevrat tsa'ar ba'alei hayyim*), Society for the Prevention of Cruelty to Animals. During World War II, the Allies were known in Hebrew as בַּעֲלוֹת הַבְּרִית (*ba'alot ha-berit*). The father of a circumcised child is also called בַּעַל בְּרִית (*ba'al berit*), probably because he and his wife are the בַּעֲלֵי שִׂמְחָה (*ba'alei simha*), hosts of the celebration. A father might boast that his daughter is not only בַּעֲלַת גִּזְרָה דְּקִיקָה (*ba'alat gizra dekika*), slim-waisted, but also בַּעֲלַת תֹּאַר דּוֹקְטוֹר (*ba'alat to'ar doktor*), a Ph.D.

And then there is the eternal verity of Jewish communal life, בַּעַל הַמֵּאָה הוּא בַּעַל הַדֵּעָה (*ba'al ha-me'ah hu ba'al ha-de'ah*), he who gives the money calls the tune. For better or worse, philanthropy is nine-tenths of ownership.

11

Gesundheit

ב-ר-א

bet-resh-alef

L eave it to Hebrew, whose speakers are thought to be indifferent to etiquette, to have two ways of saying *Gesundheit* when someone sneezes. There is לִבְרִיאוּת (*livri'ut*), to health (without a definite article)—the grammatically correct way to say it—and לַבְּרִיאוּת (*la-beri'ut*), (with the definite article), to your (literally, the) health—the way most people say it. Interestingly, Hebrew etymologists waver between two closely related roots, ב-ר-א (*bet, resh, alef*), to be fat (and, therefore, healthy), and ב-ר-ה (*bet, resh, heh*), to nourish oneself.

These roots are found in several biblical stories. There is the tale of Joseph, who interprets as seven "good" years Pharaoh's dream of seven fat cows, בְּרִיאוֹת בָּשָׂר (*beri'ot bassar*) "fleshily healthy." David's lovesick son Amnon criminally seduces his half sister Tamar by convincing her that he can recover from his listlessness only if she serves him בִּרְיָה (*biryah*), food. And then there is, from the Book of Judges, Ehud Ben-Gera, who gets away with killing the Moabite King Eglon, who was בָּרִיא מְאֹד (*bari me'od*), very fat, by burying his sword in the folds of the king's ample belly.

An example of the root's use in rabbinic literature can be found in the Aramaic prayer *Yekum Purkan,* with its straightforward petition for בַּרְיוּת גּוּפָא (*baryut gufa*), "bodily health." The term בִּרְיוֹנִים (*biryonim*), whose origin is unclear, refers to beefy Jewish Zealots fighting against the Roman occupation of Judea in the first century and is used today to designate burly bullies who abuse weaker classmates. One who does so online also has a name, בִּרְיוֹנֶט (*biryonet*), Internet bully.

Medieval philosopher-physician Maimonides advised his patients to control their lives with דְּבָרִים הַמַּבְרִין (*devarim ha-mavrin*), "nutritive things." Perhaps in a Zionist response to Rambam, Nobel

Prize writer S.Y. Agnon proclaims that the air itself of the Land of Israel is מַבְרִיא (*mavri*), "curative."

A mourner returning from the cemetery is served a סְעוּדַת הַבְרָאָה (*se'udat havra'ah*), convalescent meal. To recuperate from an illness one may repair to a בֵּית הַבְרָאָה (*beit havra'ah*) or, to use a word coined by Eliezer Ben-Yehuda, a מִבְרָאָה (*mivra'ah*), sanatorium. In the old days, one might begin a letter with a polite הִנְנִי בְּקַו הַבְּרִיאוּת (*hineni be-kav ha-beri'ut*), I am well. Today, one takes leave of a friend with a well-mannered תִּהְיֶה בָּרִיא (*tihyeh bari*), "Be well."

Etiquette? Just remember, הָעִקָּר הַבְּרִיאוּת (*ha-ikkar ha-beri'ut*), it's all good, as long as you have your health.

In the Big Inning

ב-ר-א
bet-resh-alef

I n April, everything is full of promise. It's springtime and we celebrate newly burgeoning nature. It's Passover and we rejoice at becoming a newly free nation. It's spring training and every baseball team is undefeated. And it's *Hebrew Matters* and we examine anew the story of Creation and the root ב-ר-א (*bet, resh, alef*), to create. Is Genesis 1:1 recounting that "In the beginning," God בָּרָא (*bar'a*), created the world, ex nihilo, out of nothing? Or does the text assume this and, as Rashi imagines—manipulating the vowels of the three-letter root—the Torah is reporting that Genesis begins with "Let there be light" as God בְּרֹא (*ber'o*), "goes about creating"?

Originally, the root denoted creating by cutting or carving, e.g., whittling a branch to create an arrow. More monumentally, during the conquest of Canaan, when one of the tribes complains that it is cramped for space, Joshua uses our root to reply, "Go to the forest and בָּרֵא לְךָ (*ber'e lekha*), cut down trees, to carve for yourselves an area, on which to fashion cities."

The root is found in many liturgical settings taken from Scripture. King David, having been caught dallying with Bathsheba, repents contritely, using our root to ask God, לֵב טָהוֹר בְּרָא לִי (*lev tahor ber'a li*), "Fashion a pure heart for me." In the *Yah Ribbon* Sabbath hymn, we draw on the Aramaic of the book of Daniel to chant חֵיוַת בְּרָא (*heivat ber'a*), "He created the beasts of the field." One would think that when God is called simply הַבּוֹרֵא (*ha-bor'e*), the Creator, that would cover everything. Nevertheless, among several specific Pleasure Blessings, God is also the בּוֹרֵא פְּרִי הַגֶּפֶן (*bor'e peri ha-gafen*), creator of the fruit of the vine.

Hebrew writer Haim Hazaz used our root, as it is sometimes used in Yiddish, to label a Jewish homemaker a בְּרְיָה (*biryah*), an industrious manager. In "On the Slaughter," Hayyim Nahman Bialik's poem commemorating the Kishinev Pogrom, the poet, while demanding revenge, realizes that such vengeance עוֹד לֹא בָּרָא הַשָּׂטָן (*od lo bar'a ha-satan*), "the Devil himself has not yet created." Hillel the Elder, suggesting a role model for humanity, points to Aaron the High Priest as one who אוֹהֵב אֶת הַבְּרִיאוֹת (*ohev et ha-beri'ot*), loves all God's creatures.

Today, when one categorically denies that something happened, one references Job who, according to the Talmud, לֹא הָיָה וְלֹא נִבְרָא (*lo hayah ve-lo nivra*), "neither existed nor was created."

O.K. The weather is beautiful. Go outside. It's a new inning. Play ball!

The Way of All *Fleish*

ב-שׂ-ר

bet-sin-resh

Is meat good for the Jews? The Talmud insists that every celebratory meal should consist of בָּשָׂר וְדָגִים (*basar ve-dagim*), meat and fish. But the sages of *Pirke Avot* contend that מַרְבֶּה בָּשָׂר מַרְבֶּה רִמָּה (*marbeh basar marbeh rimma*), "the more meat you eat, the more worms you have." Hebrew poses a similar quandary about meat: there are two derivatives of the root ב-שׂ-ר (*bet, sin, resh*), בָּשָׂר (*basar*), meat, and בְּשׂוֹרָה (*besora*), good tidings. Vague hints permit the conjecture that the two words are related: since the word *basar* once referred to something pleasant to the senses, one can connect eating a steak and hearing good news.

In Genesis, the word בָּשָׂר (*basar*), flesh, is initially used without carnivorous shadings. At Eve's creation from his rib, Adam exults that his companion is בָּשָׂר מִבְּשָׂרִי (*basar mi-besari*), "flesh of my flesh." Later, having acquired gluttonous cravings in the סִיר הַבָּשָׂר (*sir ha-basar*), "fleshpots," of Egypt, Israelites in the desert cry out, מִי יַאֲכִלֵנוּ בָּשָׂר (*mi ya'akhilenu basar*), "If only we had meat to eat!"

Soldiers today talk tough about death, using, for new recruits, terms like בָּשָׂר טָרִי (*basar tari*), fresh meat, and בְּשַׂר תּוֹתָחִים (*besar totahim*), cannon fodder. Often unthinkingly, writes poet Yehuda Amichai, we accept the reduction of human beings to בָּשָׂר וְדָם (*basar va-dam*), flesh and blood. To say אֲנִי בְּשָׂרִי (*ani besari*), however, means I am *fleishig,* not necessarily fleshy.

In another register, King David, not knowing what to hope for as he awaits news of his son Absalom's rebellion, sees a runner coming and cries out, גַם זֶה מְבַשֵּׂר (*gam zeh mevaser*), "He, too, brings good tidings." In a lively psalm of praise to God, David sings out, less ambiguously, בַּשְׂרוּ...יְשׁוּעָתוֹ (*basru...yeshu'ato*), "Proclaim... His victory." The prophet Isaiah provides the name for a suburb of today's Jerusalem, מְבַשֶּׂרֶת צִיוֹן (*mevaseret tsiyyon*), "herald of Zion's joy." A resident of that town, David Grossman, in his recent novel, *To the End of the Land* (Knopf)—in Hebrew, אִשָּׁה בּוֹרַחַת מִבְּשׂוֹרָה (*isha borahat mi-besora*), "A Woman Tries to Evade Bad News,"—uses the word *besora* with a negative connotation, for notifying a mother of a son's death.

The Talmud reports that during a wedding procession a כּוֹס בְּשׂוֹרָה (*kos besora*), wine cup proclaiming the bride's virginity, was carried aloft. Today, a gift shop in Tel Aviv sells a silver letter opener with בְּשׂוֹרוֹת טוֹבוֹת (*besorot tovot*), good news, engraved on the blade. Depending on the contents of the envelopes opened by the bride and groom, the letter opener is as welcome as a prime rib.

14

If Not Higher

ג-ב-ה

gimel-vet-heh

One of the lessons learned from the 2011 Israeli film *Footnote* is that when Hebrew philologists quarrel, the stakes are often more psychological than substantial. In medieval Spain, however, quarrels among grammarians could lead to charges of heresy. One hotly debated issue then was whether Hebrew roots were biliteral (two letters) or triliteral (three). Today, everybody agrees that Hebrew roots are of three letters. And yet, there are cases when one may wonder.

Take the example of ג-ב (*gimel, vet*), originally something curved, giving us the noun גַּב (*gav*), back. Add the letter נ (*nun*), and you get a rounded גִּבֵּן (*gibben*), hunchback. Curdle milk and this root will make גְּבִינָה (*gevinah*), cheese. Some say we eat cheesecake on Shavuot because rabbinic sources identified Mount Sinai with Psalms's הַר גַּבְנֻנִּים (*har gavnunnim*), a cheese-like mountain of jagged peaks.

Have you ever raked a pile of leaves? Add the letter ב (*vet*) to the two-letter root and you form גִּבֵּב (*gibbev*), to rake or pile up. The Talmud uses this root in the story of another rabbinic quarrel: the sage Eleazar Ha-Moda'i insists that the manna in the desert was piled 60 *amot* (90 feet) high. Rabbi Tarfon asks, derisively: How long will you מְגַבֵּב דְּבָרִים (*megabbev devarim*), rake up such tall stories? This story, about גּוֹבַה (*govah*), height, leads straight ג-ב-ה to (*gimel, vet, heh*), to be tall. The prophet Samuel sees future King Saul's stature as a sign, because וַיִּגְבַּה מִכָּל הָעָם (*va-yigbah mikol ha-am*), he was taller than the whole nation. God, הַמַּגְבִּיהִי לָשָׁבֶת (*ha-magbihi lashavet*), sitting on high, מַגְבִּיהַ שְׁפָלִים (*magbiah shefalim*), raises the downtrodden.

This root has been used in Jewish communal settings to "raise"—and distribute—funds. That's where we get גַּבַּאי (*gabbai*), originally, a treasurer; today, he is the fellow who distributes synagogue honors—like הַגְבָּהָה (*hagbahah*), lifting high the Torah Scroll. Interestingly, the 19th-century *pinkas* (chronicle) of Brisk, Lithuania, mentions a female גַּבָּאִית (*gabba'it*), charged with distributing to poor women "two linen dresses." California-based Magbit Foundation uses our root to provide interest-free loans for students at Israeli universities.

Error-prone computer types will want to make a גִּיבּוּי (*gibbui*), backup. A מַגְבֵּהַ (*magbe'ah*), tire jack, certainly comes in handy. At the barber, one might ask for a trim of one's rounded גַּבּוֹת (*gabbot*), eyebrows. Then there are הַחַלּוֹנוֹת הַגְּבוֹהִים (*ha-halonot ha-gevohim*), the high windows, an idiomatic expression applied to a community's higher-ups. Believe it or not, at one time this could have referred to grammarians.

15

Phoneticians Without Borders

ג-ב-ל

gimel-vet-lamed

Mountains often serve as linguistic borders; they separate languages even as they foster limited commerce between people. Curiously, but not surprisingly, if you listen carefully you'll hear how the Hebrew word גְּבוּל (*gevul*), border, and the Arabic word *jebel,* mountain, are phonetically related. To get to the Hebrew root ג-ב-ל (*gimel, vet, lamed*), to set bounds, confine, abut, one passes through its ancient meaning, to twist, and then to the braided cord, מִגְבָּלָה (*migbala*), sometimes used to delimit a territory.

At the giving of the Ten Commandments at Mount Sinai, Moses recalls God's order, הַגְבֵּל אֶת הָהָר וְקִדַּשְׁתּוֹ (*hagbel et ha-har ve-kidashto*), "Encircle the mountain and sanctify it." In Deuteronomy, the Torah's property law insists לֹא תַסִּיג גְּבוּל רֵעֶךָ (*lo tassig gevul re-akha*), "You shall not move your neighbor's boundary marker [to annex his land]." Interestingly, eight of the ten times Scripture uses the expression גְּבוּל יִשְׂרָאֵל (*gevul yisrael*), it doesn't mean the border of the land of Israel, but territory inside the border.

Modern times makes ample use of our root. First, there is the מִשְׁמָר הַגְּבוּל (*mishmar ha-gevul*), Border Patrol, a unit of the Israel Defense Forces often stationed in the territories. To protect one's personal assets one establishes a corporation with limited liability, בְּעֵרָבוֹן מוּגְבָּל (*be-eravon mugbal*), abbreviated בע"מ (*ba'am*), Ltd. Everybody has מִגְבָּלוֹת (*migbalot*), limitations, of one sort or another. Israeli society, sensitive to children who have disabilities, uses the euphemism יְלָדִים מוּגְבָּלִים (*yeladim mugbalim*), children with limitations.

When military action to the north heats up, the media will remind us that Israel...גּוֹבֶלֶת בּ (*govelet be-...*), borders on, Syria and Lebanon. A profligate person will send money לְלֹא הַגְבָּלָה (*le-lo hagbala*), without limits. One way to express anger in an argument is to shout, זֶה עוֹבֵר כָּל גְּבוּל! (*zeh over kol gevul*), that exceeds all bounds! No one will argue with the necessity to place a הַגְבָּלַת גִּיל (*hagbalat gil*), age restriction, on an R-rated movie.

Do you accept the argument that in wartime it is often necessary לְהַגְבִּיל אֶת הַזְּכוּיוֹת (*le-hagbil et ha-zekhuyot*), to limit civil rights? You might wish to protest יֵשׁ גְּבוּל! (*yesh gevul*), there are limits, you know! A stockbroker proposing a slightly risky investment warns his client that it is קְצָת גְּבוּלִי (*ketsat gevuli*), not 100 percent sure.

And then there is the 2-year-old who seems always לִבְחוֹן אֶת הַגְּבוּלוֹת (*livhon et ha-gevulot*), to test the limits his parents set on his behavior. It's important to stand firm, but don't make a mountain out of a boundary.

16

Mending Fences

ג-ד-ר

gimel-dalet-resh

When the neighbor in Robert Frost's "Mending Wall" baldly asserts, in one of American poetry's most famous verses, "Good fences make good neighbors," the poet replies subtly that neighborly goodwill might just be more fundamental than a good fence. Such is also one of the lessons learned from the Hebrew root ג-ד-ר (*gimel, dalet, resh*), fence, wall, hedge. Visitors to the northern Israeli town of Metulla learn all about הַגָּדֵר הַטּוֹבָה (*ha-gader ha-tovah*), the Good Fence, which for a time fostered cordial relations between well-intentioned residents on both sides of the border between Israel and Lebanon.

The root appears sparsely in Scripture. In one anecdote in the book of Numbers, the prophet Balaam (sent to curse Israel) is seen riding through a narrow pass, גָּדֵר מִזֶּה וְגָדֵר מִזֶּה (*gader mi-zeh ve-gader mi-zeh*), "with a fence on either side of him." Suddenly, Balaam's donkey becomes so frightened by the appearance of an angel blocking his way that he veers off the narrow path and crushes the prophet's foot against the fence. One can guess who bears the brunt of Baalam's curses at this point. Again in Numbers, when the cattle-rich tribes of Reuben and Gad ask Moses for permission to settle outside the Land of Israel proper, they argue that they need to build גִּדְרֹת צֹאן (*gidrot tson*), fenced-in sheep folds, for their livestock.

Elsewhere in Scripture, the Psalmist uses our root to introduce the term פּוֹרֵץ גָּדֵר (*porets gader*), one who metaphorically breaks through a fence, a lawbreaker. Fancifully, the Hebrew language reverses the word order of the metaphor to create the term גּוֹדֵר פֶּרֶץ (*goder perets*), one who mends a breach in a fence. Among the dozens of Canaanite towns listed in the book of Joshua as appropriate for settlement, the one called גְּדֵרֹתַיִם (*gederotayim*), literally "double fences," invites conjecture about both its linguistic and architectural structures.

Today, the reflexive verb לְהִתְגַּדֵּר (*le-hitgader*), to distinguish oneself, has both positive and negative הַגְדָּרוֹת (*hagdarot*), definitions: one may set oneself off from others by excelling at something and one may do so by obnoxiously boasting about it.

If the reader will promise not לָצֵאת מִגְּדֵרוֹ (*la-tset mi-gedero*), to lose his patience, with a far-fetched etymology, we'll conclude with the charming story of how the Hebrew word גִּדְרוֹן (*gidron*), wren—a little, sweet-singing bird often seen perched on a garden hedge—is derived from our root. According to Hungarian-born Canadian lexicographer Ernest Klein, the Hebrew word was coined by Yiddish writer Mendele Mocher Seforim, who translated it from a German expression for wren that means "king of the hedges." It turns out that good fences make good stories, too.

How Jews Stick Together

ק-ב-ד
dalet-vet-kof

In Israel, at election time, bumper stickers—from the ridiculous to the truly sublime—appear in profusion. *Stickerim* is the popular "Hebrew" word for this Israeli way of airing one's opinion. Israel's Academy of the Hebrew Language reminds us that there are perfectly suitable Hebrew alternatives derived from the root ק-ב-ד (*dalet, vet, kof*), to glue. Take, for example, מַדְבֵּקָה (*madbekah*) and תַּדְבִּיק (*tadbik*)—*both* mean gummed label—which lead to דְּבְקִית (*divkit*), sticker. The spectrum of phrases derived from our root includes דְּבֵקוּת (*devekut*), devotedness, the soul-grabbing enthusiasm one displays in prayer, as well as the "sticky-fingered" phrase דָּבֵק בְּיָדוֹ (*davek be-yado*), literally, "it sticks to his hands," referring to robbery. As we can see, the root has the advantage of adding to the discussion some wide-ranging cultural commentary.

In Scripture, the root rises to poetic heights. At the conclusion of the story of the creation of woman, the text issues an injunction that may well confer on wives a controlling hand in marriage, saying: "Therefore shall the man leave his mother and father," וְדָבַק בְּאִשְׁתּוֹ (*ve-davak be-ishto*), "and cleave unto his wife." In the biblical oath of allegiance to Jerusalem from Psalm 137, one swears: תִּדְבַּק לְשׁוֹנִי לְחִכִּי (*tidbak leshoni le-hikki*), "May my tongue cleave to my palate, [if I do not remember you]."

The root is found multiple times in the story of Ruth, who is called by the rabbis הַדְּבוּקָה (*ha-devukah*), the one who became attached to the Jewish people. After the death of Naomi's sons, one daughter-in-law separates herself from Naomi, while Ruth דָּבְקָה בָּה (*davka ba*), clung to her. Back in Bethlehem, kindhearted Boaz invites a destitute Ruth to glean from his fields, suggesting, תִּדְבָּקִין עִם נַעֲרֹתָי (*tidbakin im na'arotai*), "stick with my girls." In a less glorious incident described in the Bible, namely the death of King

Saul, the prophet Samuel recounts the story of the Philistines who—giving the root two meanings—וַיִּדְבְּקוּ...אֶת שָׁאוּל (*va-yidbeku...et sha'ul*), both pursued and caught Saul.

The noun דֶּבֶק (*devek*) means glue, except when it doesn't. Sometimes it refers to a nudnik (who gets on another's nerves and won't let go) or, alluding to *davak* in the story of the creation of woman, to a prospective groom. The term דִּבּוּק (*dibbuk*), incubus, calls to mind the play by Yiddish playwright S. Ansky that tells of a demon that clings to the soul of a suffering bride.

Bumper *stickerim*—like life—teach us that not all stickiness is helpful. But when love of Hebrew becomes מְדַבֵּק (*medabbek*), infectious, it's all to the good.

18

That's What the Last Minute Is For

ד-ק-ק
dalet-kof-kof

There are two types of people in this world: דַּיְקָנִים (*daykanim*), those obsessed with accuracy and punctuality; and those who arrive casually at the דַּקָּה הַתִּשְׁעִים (*dakka ha-tish'im*), 90th minute (the last minute of a soccer match). Both expressions derive from ד-ק-ק (*dalet, kof, kof*), originally to pulverize or grind to a thin powder. In the biblical story of the Golden Calf, Moses, enraged, burns the statue, then וַיִּטְחַן עַד אֲשֶׁר דָּק (*va-yithan ad asher dak*), "grinds it thoroughly." Mixing the thin powder with water, he makes the Israelites drink it. In Pharaoh's dreams, cows and sheaves of wheat are דַּקּוֹת (*dakkot*), emaciated or withered. The book of Kings uses the adjective metaphorically when it describes the קוֹל דְּמָמָה דַקָּה (*kol demama dakka*), "thin small voice," heard by the prophet Elijah as he flees the wrath of Jezebel. One of the most lyrical of Isaiah's prophecies uses our root to praise God the creator, הַנּוֹטֶה כַדֹּק שָׁמַיִם (*ha-noteh kha-dok shamayim*), "who spreads out the skies like gauze."

In rabbinic literature, a דְּקָקָה (*dekaka*), is a tender child, while בְּהֵמָה דַקָּה (*behema daka*), denotes small cattle. During the preparation of incense for the Temple ritual, the priest grinding it, or his supervisor, would chant repeatedly הָדֵק הֵיטֵב (*hadek hetev*), "Grind it very thoroughly!"—implying that the sound of a voice is somehow beneficial to the incense itself. The root also serves clinical purposes, using the same word, דַּקִּים (*dakkim*), for small intestines and, euphemistically perhaps, urination. Medically, דֹּק (*dok*) denotes a cataract. Concerned with digestive health, the rabbis urged the populace דּוֹק בַּשִּׁנַּיִם (*dok ba-shinnayim*), chew your food thoroughly.

The Talmud states that God, harsher with the very pious, מְדַקְדֵּק עִם סְבִיבָיו (*medakdek im sevivav*), demands stricter observance from those closest to Him. In language matters, medieval grammarian Menahem ben Saruk is among the first to use the word דִּקְדּוּק (*dikduk*), fine point, to mean, simply, grammar.

In a subtle play on words, the letter ע (*ayin*) in the expression דִּקְדּוּקֵי עֲנִיּוּת (*dikdukei aniyyut*), crushing poverty, is changed to an א (*alef*), as in אֲנִי (*ani*), ego, giving us דִּקְדּוּקֵי אֲנִיּוּת (*dikdukei aniyyut*), petty self-centeredness. Where this expression comes from בְּדִיּוּק (*be-diyyuk*), precisely, is unclear but, דַּוְקָא (*davka*), just so, it provides us with a fine pun.

Precision is fine but, as linguist Reuven Sivan warns, beware of דַּיְקָנוּת נוּקְשָׁה (*daykanut nuksha*), too rigid exactitude. We all know that "I'll be ready in חֲצִי דַּקָּה (*hatsi dakka*)," half a minute, often translates into 15 minutes. This gives us plenty of time to read about the fine points of the Hebrew language.

19

Jews for Exegesis

ד-ר-שׁ

dalet-resh-shin

O ften, words will leave the comfortable world of their plain, concrete meaning and soar into the realm of metaphor. Take, for example, the Hebrew root ד-ר-שׁ (*dalet, resh, shin*), to explicate. Originally, it was based on an agricultural term for separating the wheat from the chaff, ד-ר-ס (*dalet, resh, samekh*), to trample, thresh. Soon enough, the new root was used figuratively to describe the way the rabbis of the Talmud would search for the deeper meaning of a biblical text.

In Scripture, the root is found in a wide variety of contexts. Proverbs praises the woman of valor for her industriousness, stating, דָּרְשָׁה צֶמֶר וּפִשְׁתִּים (*darsha tzemer u-phishtim*), "she sought out wool and flax." In II Kings, the Israelite King Ahazia instructs his servants to דִּרְשׁוּ בְּבַעַל זְבוּב (*dirshu be-va'al zevuv*), "inquire of Beelzebub," a local god, whether Ahazia will recover from life-threatening wounds suffered from his fall off a balcony. The Prophet Elijah, learning of this blasphemy, intercepts the servants on the way to their task and harshly informs them that the king will not recover. The Prophet Micah asks the ultimate question, מָה ה' דּוֹרֵשׁ מִמְּךָ (*mah ha-shem doresh mi-mekha*), "What does God demand of you?" before answering sublimely: "Do justice, love goodness and walk modestly with your God."

A familiar derivative of our root is the word מִדְרָשׁ (*midrash*), explication, which has meanings all over the lexical map. The midrash is the part of the oral Torah that explains problematic or unclear passages of the written Torah by telling didactic parables. Our elders teach that לֹא הַמִּדְרָשׁ הָעִקָּר (*lo ha-midrash ha-ikkar*), "study is less central than acts." Other usages of the root include דַּרְשָׁן (*darshan*), exegete, and דְּרַשׁ (*derash*), homiletical exegesis. Many synagogues have an adjoining בֵּית מִדְרָשׁ (*beit midrash*), study hall.

The term מִדְרָשָׁה (*midrasha*), coined by Eliezer Ben-Yehuda, connotes a post-secondary school for Jewish studies. The cognate Arabic *madrassa* is a school that teaches Islamic texts.

Come fall in Israel, you'll see flyers announcing דְּרוּשָׁה מְטַפֶּלֶת (*derushah metapelet*), "Nanny Wanted." During Israeli summers, there is very little דְּרִישָׁה (*derishah*), demand, for umbrellas. Capital cases call for דְּרִישָׁה וַחֲקִירָה (*derisha ve-hakira*), painstaking legal investigation. Casual conversations will often end with the plain-sounding abbreviation דָּ"ש (*dash*), "Regards," shorthand for the poetic expression דְּרִישַׁת שָׁלוֹם (*derishat shalom*), literally, plea for peace—a good way to end a column as well.

20

Have You Heard the Buzz?

ה-ג-ה
heh-gimel-heh

Y our elbow on your knee, your chin in your hand, you sit staring at the blank computer screen. Gradually, an image of Rodin's *The Thinker* emerges, slowly lifting its head and mumbling. Our הוֹגֶה דֵעוֹת (*hogeh de'ot*), philosopher, murmurs words that use the Hebrew root ה-ג-ה (*heh, gimel, heh*), to meditate, to murmur. He goes on to philosophize about lions growling, pigeons cooing and humans reasoning, all from the same root.

In Scripture, the psalmist laments כִּלִּינוּ שָׁנֵינוּ כְמוֹ הֶגֶה (*killinu shaneinu khemo hegeh*), "our lives end like a fleeting murmur." He also uses our root in הִגָּיוֹן בְּכִנּוֹר (*higgayon be-khinor*), lyre music, and הֶגְיוֹן לִבִּי (*hegyon libi*), the heart's meditation.

Medieval grammarian David Kimchi, the Radak, associates our root with a Jewish value. He declares that the expression in Psalms, וּבְתוֹרָתוֹ יֶהְגֶּה יוֹמָם וָלָיְלָה (*u-ve-torato yehgeh yomam va-laila*), does not mean merely "one should study His Torah day and night." Radak insists that *yehgeh* means murmur, that one should be so immersed in Torah study that even when one nods off one should mumble its words involuntarily. The Deuteronomy Rabba commentary makes a distinction between הוֹגֶיהָ (*hogeha*) and עוֹשֶׂיהָ (*oseha*), those who study the law and those who do it. In tractate Berakhot the Talmud warns מִנְעוּ בְּנֵיכֶם מִן הַהִגָּיוֹן (*min'u beneikhem min ha-higgayon*), "restrain your children from superficial parroting of the Bible." In tractate Sanhedrin one is admonished not to be a הוֹגֶה אֶת הַשֵּׁם בְּאוֹתִיוֹתָיו (*hogeh et ha-shem be-otiotav*), "one who pronounces the Divine Name as It is written." Rather, as in the Days of Awe liturgy, God should be הֶהָגוּי בְּאֶהְיֶה אֲשֶׁר אֶהְיֶה (*he-hagui be-ehyeh asher ehyeh*), "One whose name is pronounced, 'I am that I am.'"

Today, the root is applied to one of the neglected Hebrew arts, תּוֹרַת הַהֲגוּי (*torat ha-higui*), phonetics. There one learns of הֶגֶה אָטוּם, קוֹלִי אוֹ אַפִּי (*hegeh atum, koli o api*), a consonant that is unvoiced, voiced or nasal.

A popular admonition is אַל תּוֹצִיא הֶגֶה מִפִּיךְ (*al totsi hegeh mi-pikha*), don't utter a sound. Speaking of don't, don't confuse *hegeh,* utterance, with *hegeh,* steering wheel, from a different root. And speaking of different roots, don't confuse הֲגִיָּה (*hagiyya*), pronunciation, with הַגָּהָה (*haggaha*), proofreading, from נ-ג-ה (*nun, gimel, heh*), to throw light upon. This distinction נִשְׁמַע הֶגְיוֹנִי (*nishma hegyoni*), sounds logical. Even the person who הָרָה וְהָגָה (*hara ve-haga*), thought up this discussion, agrees: anything is more *hegyoni* than a statue coming to life on a computer screen.

21

To Be—That Is the Answer

ה-י-ה

heh-yod-heh

Ask the Prince of Denmark whether "to be" or not and he will hem and haw. Ask the King of Kings a similar question and He will reply, אֶהְיֶה אֲשֶׁר אֶהְיֶה (*eheyeh asher eheyeh*), I am and always will be. The root ה-י-ה (*heh, yod, heh*), to be, become, remain and its alternate spelling, ה-ו-ה (*heh, vav, heh*), are found more than 3,500 times in Scripture. The first word out of God's mouth in Genesis is יְהִי (*yehi*), "Let there be." As Rebekah takes leave of her family to marry Isaac, they bless her with הֱיִי לְאַלְפֵי רְבָבָה (*hayi le-alfei revava*), "May you become [the mother of] myriads." In Deuteronomy, God's promise is fulfilled with the assertion הַיּוֹם הַזֶּה נִהְיֵיתָ לְעָם (*ha-yom ha-zeh niheyeta le-am*), "Today you became a nation."

The composers of the liturgy used the biblical expression וַיְהִי עֶרֶב וַיְהִי בֹקֶר (*va-yehi erev va-yehi voker*), "There was evening, there was morning," to introduce the Friday evening Kiddush. In *Pirke Avot* we frequently find the expression הוּא הָיָה אוֹמֵר (*hu haya omer*), "He used to say." And God's Ineffable Name—which we don't pronounce—is carefully identified as שֵׁם הַהֲוָיָה (*shem ha-havayah*), literally, the Name of Existence.

Hayyim Nahman Bialik used our root to coin the word הֲוַי (*havai*) to describe a people's way of life—its customs, culture, and manners. An idiomatic quirk of the root occurs when one considers the two meanings of the word אִישׁ (*ish*), man or husband. Thus, הָיָה לְאִישׁ (*haya le-ish*) is he became manly, and הָיְתָה לְאִישׁ (*hayeta le-ish*), she got married.

While Ecclesiastes preached מַה שֶּׁהָיָה הוּא שֶׁיִּהְיֶה (*mah she-haya hu she-yiheyeh*), "What has been is that which shall be," a modern Israeli will more likely say, מַה שֶּׁהָיָה—הָיָה (*mah she-haya—haya*), what was—was, i.e., don't cry over spilt milk. The root is often doubled to introduce a story, as in הָיֹה הָיוּ שְׁנֵי חֲבֵרִים (*hayo hayu shenei haverim*), once there were two friends.

Did your friend apply for a job? הֱיוֹת וְאַתָּה שׁוֹאֵל (*heyot ve-ata sho'el*), since you are asking, I will tell you that הָיָה לוֹ לִשְׁלוֹחַ קוֹרוֹת חַיִּים (*haya lo lishlo'ah korot hayyim*), he should have sent in his résumé, rather than just call the company on the telephone. Anyway, הָיוּ אִתּוֹ עִנְיָנִים (*hayu itto inyan-im*), there were "issues" with him, and לֹא יָכוֹל לִהְיוֹת (*lo yakhol liheyot*), it's not possible, that he was hired.

If you are the nostalgic type, the words הָיוּ זְמַנִּים (*hayu zemanim*), those were the days, will often be found on your lips. If you are like me, you will end every conversation with תִּהְיֶה בָּרִיא (*tiheyeh bari*), stay healthy.

22

From a Hum to a Howl

ה-מ-ה
heh-mem-heh

When forefather Abram is awarded the name Abraham, the Torah's etymological explanation is that he will one day become אָב הֲמוֹן גּוֹיִם (*av hamon goyim*), "father of many nations." Today's etymologists remind us that הֲמוֹן (*hamon*) derives from the root ה-מ-ה (*heh, mem, heh*). If you sound out the verb הוֹמֶה (*homeh*), you will hear a modest onomatopoetic "hum," like the הֶמְיָה (*hemya*), cooing, of a dove. Intensify this hum, using the related root ה-מ-מ (*heh, mem, mem*), and you will go from a near-silent murmur to a noisy howl, as in מְהוּמָה (*mehumah*), commotion. Scripture has many gradations between these two extremes.

In Song of Songs, the beloved's heart is so stirred מֵעַי הָמוּ עָלָיו (*me'ai hamu alav*), "my intestines moan over him." In Psalm 39, it is futile that people יֶהֱמָיוּן (*yehemayun*), should "bustle" about. And then there is blood-thirsty Jezebel and a drought. Elijah appears to Jezebel's husband, Ahab, and conjures up for him the sound of הֲמוֹן הַגֶּשֶׁם (*hamon ha-gashem*), the rumbling sound of approaching rain.

While this column does not always endeavor to speak to the הֲמוֹנִים (*ha-monim*), masses, it does try to contribute to the הִמּוּן (*himmun*), popularization, of Hebrew language and literature. Hayyim Nahman Bialik, in a popular Zionist poem, sings of בַּת יוֹנִים הוֹמִיָּה (*bat yonim homiyyah*), a cooing dove, that leads a young boy in a rowboat to the promised land but does not gain him entry. Israeli writer Meir Shalev, in his novel *A Pigeon and a Boy,* uses Bialik's poem as the springboard for a story about the War of Independence. The boy, plucked from Bialik's rowboat, is now helping the war effort by the use of a well-trained יוֹנָה הוֹמִיָּה (*yonah homiyyah*), which—playing on *homeh* and home—some commentators have taken the liberty to translate as "homing pigeon."

There are two Israeli הִימְנוֹנִים (*himnonim*, from Greek *hymnos*, not our root despite appearances), anthems, associated with a form of our root. "*Hatikvah*" sings of נֶפֶשׁ יְהוּדִי הוֹמִיָּה (*nefesh yehudi homiyyah*), "the yearning Jewish heart," always looking to Zion, while "*Shir Ha-Palmach*" sings of its courageous soldiers, whose head is not bowed while מִסָּבִיב יֶהֹם הַסַּעַר (*mi-saviv yehom ha-sa'ar*), "all around the storm does rage."

Even Shakespeare gets into the act. The Hebrew expression הַרְבֵּה מְהוּמָה עַל לֹא מְאוּמָה (*harbeh mehumah al lo me'umah*) is a translation of his *Much Ado About Nothing.* Yet even Shakespeare would have to agree that to get from a hum to a howl to Abraham's multitudes is worthy of much ado.

23

Careful! Words at Play

ז-ה-ר
zayin-heh-resh

For medieval Hebrew etymologists as well as for the folks at Merriam-Webster, some words, like children, just want to get out and play. Take the example of the Hebrew root ז-ה-ר (*zayin, heh, resh*), which presents a fascinating enigma. The authoritative *Brown-Driver-Briggs* lexicon of biblical Hebrew leaves it to us to conjecture how we get from "shining," the root's original sense, to the notion of "warning," its subsequent usage.

In Scripture, the root appears twice in one verse of the book of Daniel; in 12:3, the angel Michael prophesies that when the dead are resurrected, the "enlightened" יַזְהִירוּ כְּזֹהַר הָרָקִיעַ (*yazhiru ke-zohar ha-rakia*), "will be radiant like the bright expanse of the sky." It is not insignificant that our root appears 18 times in the book of Ezekiel, the prophet of the heavenly chariot. In his vision, Ezekiel is confronted with a מַרְאֵה זֹהַר (*mar'eh zohar*), a radiant figure having the appearance of fire. Today, the word זוֹהַר (*zohar*) is used to describe the splendor of nature's Aurora Borealis. These connections are especially striking when we recall that the foundational text of the Kabbalah is סֵפֶר הַזֹּהַר (*sefer ha-zohar*), the Book of Splendor, a mystical text often attributed to Shimon bar Yohai—the rabbi we celebrate with Lag B'Omer bonfires. The Talmud's זַהֲרוּרֵי הַחַמָּה (*zaharurei ha-hammah*), the glowing red streak of the setting sun, bridges bright day to ominous night.

In other rabbinic texts, different senses of the root appear, for example in the talmudic admonition הִזָּהֲרוּ בִּבְנֵי עֲנִיִּים (*hizaharu bivnei aniim*), "Take care of the children of the poor" because they are where Torah will come from. In Jewish law, a sinner may be punished only if הִזְהִירוּ אוֹתוֹ (*hizhiru oto*), he was forewarned of the prohibition. *Pirke Avot* warns our Sages themselves to הִזָּהֲרוּ בְּדִבְרֵיכֶם (*hizaharu be-divreikhem*), "Be careful with your words."

In Israel, if you are in the proximity of high voltage, you may come upon a red triangle enclosing an exclamation point. The accompanying word, אַזְהָרָה (*azharah*), warning, tells you to be זָהִיר (*zahir*), cautious, of the danger. Similarly, roadblock signs read זְהִירוּת (*zehirut*), "Careful!" In other expansions of the root, there is the brilliant child with an עָתִיד מַזְהִיר (*atid mazhir*), promising future, and the gleaming נַעֲרַת זֹהַר (*na'arat zohar*), glamour girl. Even further from its root, זְהוֹרִית (*zehorit*), rayon, refers to the fabric's shiny sheen .

O.K. A quick warning to all those still seeking enlightenment about our root—playtime is over.

24

The Merit System

ז-כ-ה
zayin-khof-heh

ז-כ-ה
zayin-khof-heh

S ome people like to say that Israel is a country that runs on Vitamin P. They are referring to the embrace of *protektzia* by the early settlers, where זְכוּיוֹת (*zekhuyyot*), benefits, were said to be doled out by nepotism. For others, Israel is a true meritocracy, where כָּל הַקּוֹדֵם זָכָה (*kol ha-kodem zakha*), first come, first served. In both cases, the student of Hebrew will encounter ז-כ-ה (*zayin, khof, heh*), to merit, a many-nuanced root having to do with clarity, purity and innocence.

Sometimes, to get at the root of a Hebrew root, it pays to look at its two-letter version. Here it means purity, as in the biblical requirement that the Tabernacle's Eternal Lamp use only שֶׁמֶן זַיִת זַךְ (*shemen zayit zakh*), pure olive oil. The word *zakh* is used with a moral undertone by Job who, protesting his innocence, proclaims זַךְ אֲנִי בְּלִי פָשַׁע (*zakh ani beli fasha*), "I am pure, without sin." For Job, to be pure is to be innocent.

Rabbi Hananiah ben Akashia, a talmudic sage, wanted to know why there are so many mitzvot. He concluded that God wanted לְזַכּוֹת אֶת יִשְׂרָאֵל (*le-zakkot et yisrael*), to provide the Israelites with as many opportunities as possible to earn merit. Indeed, when the charity collector leaves, he doesn't say thank you; rather, he blesses you with תִּזְכֶּה לְמִצְוֹת (*tizkeh le-mitzvot*), may you merit to perform even more righteous deeds. In Aramaic, *zakha* is related to צֶדֶק (*tzedek*), justice. In Islam, *zakka* is another word for *tzedaka*, charity.

Uses of our root in Jewish history and practice include the name of Rabbi Yohanan ben Zakkai, the man credited with preserving Judaism after the destruction of Jerusalem, and the name of the prayer recited before Yom Kippur, תְּפִלָּה זַכָּה (*tefilla zakka*), that exonerates one's acquaintances for any damages they may have caused one during the previous year.

If you look conscientiously through a transparent pane of זְכוּכִית (*zekhukhit*), glass, you might, like medieval grammarian David Kimchi, see a crystal-clear relationship to our root.

In the literary world, writer Meir Shalev זָכָה בְּפְרָס (*zakha bi-feras*), won a prize, for his novel, *A Pigeon and a Boy* (Schocken). In business circles, one can gain an exclusive right to develop a piece of public property, such as a radio station, by acquiring a זִכָּיוֹן (*zikkayon*), concession.

Some will say that such a זְכוּת (*zekhut*), legal right, is often acquired only by those who have *protektzia*. Others will insist that each of us is בְּחֶזְקַת זַכַּאי (*be-hezkat zakkai*), presumed innocent, and that first come, first served is a virtuous principle indeed.

25

I Threw a Word in the Air...

ז-ר-ק
zayin-resh-kof

What do Moses, urban planners, health professionals, strict teachers, and Torah chanters have in common? Well, if you throw these words into the air—along with a dozen more—they will fall to earth in the vicinity of the Hebrew root ז-ר-ק (*zayin, resh, kof*), to throw, sprinkle.

In Scripture, the root has several distinct meanings. In Leviticus, priests are ordered to זָרְקוּ אֶת הַדָּם (*zarku et ha-dam*), sprinkle sacrificial blood (against the altar walls), using a special מִזְרָק (*mizrak*), bowl. In Egypt, Moses is charged to take a handful of soot וּזְרָקוֹ...הַשָּׁמַיְמָה (*u-zerako...hashamaimah*) and throw it toward the sky; when it falls to earth, it brings on the sixth plague—boils. In a strange linguistic twist, the prophet Hosea, using a bakery metaphor, compares sinful Israel to a rotting cake, on which שֵׂיבָה זָרְקָה (*seivah zarkah*), mold (some say, "gray hair") is scattered. Legendary 20th-century Bible educator Nechama Leibovitz was reputed to have a disciplinary quirk: if you came to her class without a bible text in hand, נְחָמָה זוֹרֶקֶת (*nehama zoreket*), the beloved teacher would throw you out.

The Talmud uses our root allegorically, to teach discernment. One should eat the nutritious part of the fruit, to be sure, but קְלִפָּתוֹ זוֹרֵק (*kelipato zorek*), throw away the unpalatable peel. Tractate Hullin, for its part, warns of unintended consequences. Do not be like one who, thinking he's doing a righteous act, זוֹרֵק אֶבֶן לְמֶרְקוֹלִיס (*zorek even le-merkolis*), throws a stone at a pagan statue of Mercury, because, unknowingly, he is committing idol worship. When medieval Masoretic scribes created a system of musical cantillation for the public chanting of the Torah, they used the Aramaic word זַרְקָא (*zarka*) to indicate a "scattering" of five different notes. In an orchestra, string instruments have a pair of זְרְקָתַיִם (*zarkatayyim*), sound holes, through which the violin's music resonates.

Today, a health care worker at the clinic will fill a מַזְרֵק (*mazrek*), syringe, with תַּזְרִיק (*tazrik*), serum, to administer a זְרִיקָה (*zerikah*), injection. In scornful slang, a זָרוּק (*zaruk*) is a drug addict. To project light distantly, use the portmanteau word זַרְקוֹר (*zarkor*), light thrower, i.e., searchlight. In 2015, urban planners in Eilat installed a flashy מִזְרָקָה (*mizrakah*), ornamental fountain, called the Musical Fountain, which sprinkles water, light and music on tourists. Then there is the tiresome זוֹרֵק שֵׁמוֹת (*zorek sheimot*), name dropper, as well as the colleague who asks you לִזְרוֹק מִלָּה (*lizrok millah*), to throw in a good word with the boss. As for this column, לֹא לִזְרוֹק (*lo lizrok*), don't throw it in the trash. It contains much Hebrew nourishment.

26

When Israel Celebrates

ח-ג-ג
het-gimel-gimel

The debate had been raging now for months: Should the 60th anniversary of the State of Israel be celebrated with solemn reserve or wild revelry? Not coincidentally, the root ח-ג-ג (*het, gimel, gimel*), to celebrate, contains both nuances. Thus, then Israeli President Shimon Peres might have announced חֲגִיגִית (*hagigit*), solemnly, a celebratory חֲגִיגָה (*hagiga*), festival, on 3 Iyyar (moved back from the 5th because of Shabbat).

Early on, the root meant to leap or dance and, therefore, to turn in circles. In Scripture, when David confronts the Amalekites who had burned the town of Ziklag to the ground, he is distressed to find them in a celebratory mood—eating, drinking, וְחֹגְגִים (*ve-hogegim*), "and making merry." More soberly, Moses informs Pharaoh that God insists that the Israelites leave Egypt so that יָחֹגּוּ לִי (*yahoggu li*), "they will sacrifice to Me." Hagiga is also the name of a tractate of Talmud, dealing with festival sacrifice—represented on the Seder plate, for example, by a "circular" egg.

The word חַג (*hag*), festival, is attached to all the pilgrimage festivals in the Torah, circular, perhaps, because they take place periodically. Sukkot, a particularly joyous holiday, is called הֶחָג (*he-hag*), the holiday, par excellence. Interestingly, according to scholars, the Arabic word *haj*, the Muslim pilgrimage to Mecca, is a direct borrowing from the Hebrew word *hag*.

While the prophet Amos states מָאַסְתִּי חַגֵּיכֶם (*ma'asti haggeikhem*), "I despise your feast offerings," the psalmist declares no less emphatically that holidays be celebrated by הָמוֹן חוֹגֵג (*hamon hogeg*), "vast numbers of celebrants." That Jewish festivals are to be celebrated joyfully is found in Deuteronomy's וְשָׂמַחְתָּ בְּחַגֶּיךָ (*ve-samahta be-haggekha*), "Rejoice on your festivals," and in the festival Kiddush, חַגִּים וּזְמַנִּים לְשָׂשׂוֹן (*haggim u-zemannim le-sasson*), "the holidays and times for joy."

The related root, ח-ו-ג (*het, vav, gimel*), to encircle, is found in a Hebrew version of "Ring Around the Rosy." The song tells children בַּמַּעְגָּל נָחוּגָה (*ba-ma'agal nahugga*), let us dance around in a circle. This root has also morphed into an appropriate meeting place for Hebrew lovers, the חוּג עִבְרִית (*hug ivrit*), Hebrew circle.

If only to celebrate with Hebrew in May, put on a תִּלְבּוֹשֶׁת חֲגִיגִית (*til-boshet hagigit*), party frock, and make the day חֲגִיגָה לָעֵינַיִם (*hagiga la-eina-yim*), a feast for the eyes. After all, בְּכָל יוֹם חַג לֹא (*lo bekhol yom hag*), not every day is a holiday.

27

Holey, Holey, Holey

ח-ל-ל
het-lamed-lamed

No one is quite sure where the challa on your Shabbat table comes from: the word, that is, not the loaf. It may be derived from the root ח-ל-ה (*het, lamed, heh*), sweetness, as in the Middle Eastern treat חַלְוָה (*halva*), or as in חַלַּת דְּבַשׁ (*hallat devash*), honeycomb. Halla—what Rashi's commentary on Numbers 15:20 calls, in Old French, a "little torte"—is sweeter than rye bread, *n'est-ce pas?*

But what about the notice on the side of a box of *matzot* in the pantry assuring us that חַלָּה (*halla*) has been taken out? Quite possibly, that word is rooted in ח-ל-ל (*het, lamed, lamed*), to hollow out, because when one "takes halla"—i.e., a portion of a batch of dough taken originally as a priestly offering—one creates a hollow.

Initially, our root meant to turn round and round, to bore a hole. That's how we get the word חָלָל (*halal*), one who dies in battle, because formerly soldiers died when they were "holey," pierced by a sword.

On a happier note, the root gives us מָחוֹל (*mahol*), circle dance. And then there is the expression וְחוֹזֵר חֲלִילָה (*ve-hozer halilah*), and so on, that also implies circularity. Let us also not forget that כָּל הַתְחָלוֹת קָשׁוֹת (*kol hat'halot kashot*), all beginnings are difficult (a beginning is also a cutting out). Shabbat may have been created last but according to the *"Lekha Dodi"* hymn chanted on Friday evening, Shabbat was בְּמַחֲשָׁבָה תְּחִלָּה (*be-mahashavah tehillah*), in God's mind from the very beginning.

A יוֹם חֹל (*yom hol*), weekday, describes an absence of holiness. And חֹל הַמּוֹעֵד (*hol ha-mo'ed*) is the intermediate days of a holiday. Today, a significant portion of Israeli society are חִלּוֹנִים (*hillonim*), secularists.

Scripture tells us that Noah looked out of a חַלּוֹן (*hallon*), an opening in the ark, i.e., window, to verify whether the Flood was abating. Nowadays, the word *hallon* is used to signify the wedge of watermelon the merchant cuts out to let the customer verify its quality (and sweetness?). It's also a bank teller's window or a computer screen. When one of the firm's חַלּוֹנוֹת הַגְּבוֹהִים (*hallonot ha-gevohim*), literally, high windows, and figuratively, big shots at the top, has a *hallon* in his day between appointments, he'll be glad to see you.

Nobody wants to commit a חִלּוּל הַשֵּׁם (*hillul ha-shem*), desecration of God's name. We could stop on that note but חַס וְחָלִילָה (*has ve-halilah*), Heaven forbid, we should omit the חָלִיל (*halil*), recorder, that quintessentially Israeli hollowed-out musical instrument.

Its sound is as sweet as a Shabbat loaf.

28

Keep the Change

ח-ל-פ
het-lamed-feh

Former President George W. Bush warned that extremist Muslims were preparing to reestablish the caliphate and institute totalitarian regimes worldwide. In so doing, beyond radical politics, they would also be getting into Hebrew etymology. In traditional Islam, the caliph—in Arabic, *khalifa*; in Hebrew, חָלִיף (*halif*)—is the successor of the Prophet Muhammad, his stand-in. The Hebrew word derives from the root, ח-ל-פ (*het, lamed, feh*), to change, exchange or pass through.

The root appears at critical moments in Scripture. In Genesis, Jacob complains that his father-in-law repeatedly הֶחֱלִיף אֶת מַשְׂכֻּרְתִּי (*hehelif et maskurti*), "changed my wages." When Joseph learns that he is to be released from prison, וַיְחַלֵּף שִׂמְלֹתָיו (*va-yehallef simlotav*), "he changes his clothes." In Numbers, the Levites are promised a tithe חֵלֶף עֲבוֹדָתָם (*helef avodatam*), "in exchange for their work" in the sanctuary. The lovers in the Song of Songs report joyfully הַגֶּשֶׁם חָלָף (*ha-geshem halaf*), "the [winter] rain has passed." The most problematic use of our root in Scripture comes from the story of Samson, as he explains to Delilah that his מַחְלְפוֹת (*mahlafot*), "plaits of hair," are his weak point. One scholar conjectures that braiding involves one plait passing through another.

Another difficulty is the rabbinic use of the noun חַלָּף (*hallaf*) for a ritual slaughterer's knife, which—might we speculate?—passes rapidly through the flesh of the animal. The rabbis use our root metaphorically to warn against making a bad deal, לְהַחֲלִיף פָּרָה בַּחֲמוֹר (*le-hahalif para ba-hamor*), to exchange a cow for a donkey. In the *Kapparot* ceremony used to ward off the evil decree before Yom Kippur, one recites the formula זֶה חֲלִיפָתִי (*zeh halifati*), "This [chicken or money] shall be my substitute."

Today, one buys a new חֲלִיפָה (*halifa*), suit, for the holidays. By email, or לַחֲלוּפִין (*la-halufin*), alternatively, by post, some people carry on a חֲלִיפַת מִכְתָּבִים (*halifat mikhtavim*), correspondence. A basketball team has five starters and five מַחְלִיפִים (*mahlifim*), substitutes. At the grocery you may buy margarine as a תַּחְלִיף (*tahlif*), substitute, for butter. To exit the highway, you look for the appropriate מֶחְלָף (*mehlaf*), interchange. At the lab, you examine the חִלּוּפִית (*hillufit*), amoeba, to note its changes of shape. In trading cards, a lucky youngster has plenty of הַחְלָפוֹת (*hahlafot*), doubles, to exchange. And you go to the חַלְפָן (*halfan*), moneychanger, to buy shekels at the going שַׁעַר חֲלִיפִין (*sha'ar halifin*), exchange rate. Finally, in times of anxiety the most calming words are חָלְפָה הַסַּכָּנָה (*halfa ha-sakkana*), the danger is past. *Inshalla*.

29

At the Campfire

ח-נ-ה

het-nun-heh

W hat does the study of Jewish and Zionist culture have to do with ball playing? For one thing, both activities can be found at Young Judaea's several מַחֲנוֹת קַיִץ (*mahanot kayitz*), summer camps, across the United States. Not incidentally, the Hebrew root from which מַחֲנֶה (*mahaneh*) derives, ה-נ-ח (*het, nun, heh*), to encamp, is also tied to both recreational activities and Jewish history.

The original meaning of the root, to bend or incline, can be deduced from an expression in the book of Judges, הִנֵּה חֲנוֹת הַיּוֹם (*hineh hanot ha-yom*), "Behold the day [i.e., the sun] bends" toward its resting place. The modern word חָנוּת (*hanut*), shop, comes from our root. It is recorded that the prophet Jeremiah was imprisoned in חֲנֻיּוֹת (*hanuyot*), vaulted chambers. Subsequently, a חָנוּת (*hanut*), little cell with an arched roof, was used by חֶנְוָנִים (*henvanim*), shopkeepers, to do business.

In Scripture, the noun *mahaneh* means not only encampment where people rest but also army—בַּמַּחֲנֶה (*ba-mahaneh*) is the title of the Israel Defense Forces' periodical—or, as in Jacob's funeral, מַחֲנֶה כָּבֵד מְאֹד (*mahaneh kaved me'od*), "large horde of people." By adding the preposition עַל (*al*), against, to the verb, the Bible changes the meaning from "resting" to something more warlike. In II Samuel, David is exhorted, חֲנֵה עַל הָעִיר (*haneh al ha-ir*), "besiege the city." And the psalmist proclaims אִם תַּחֲנֶה עָלַי מַחֲנֶה (*im tahaneh alai mahaneh*), "should an army besiege me," I would have no fear.

According to medieval etymologists, חֲנִית (*hanit*), spear, also derives somehow from our root. Did not Isaiah prophesy that חֲנִיתוֹתֵיהֶם (*hanitoteihem*), their spears, would be ground into pruning hooks, ushering in eternal rest from war?

Moses sends scouts to Canaan to check whether the locals live בְּמַחֲנִים (*be-mahanim*), in unguarded camps. Today, מַחֲנַיִם (*mahanayim*), literally meaning two camps, is a version of dodge ball, a game often played by מַחֲנָאִים (*mahana'im*), campers.

A base in Israeli softball, תַּחֲנָה (*tahana*), is also a station. Until the train comes, there is always the problem of parking one's car. When you are tempted not to feed the מַדְחָן (*madhan*), parking meter, or to ignore the אֵין חֲנָיָה (*ein hanaya*), no parking, sign, don't risk it; the fines are outrageous.

All these issues—from biblical warfare to modern Israeli laws—are fuel for discussion at the campfires of Young Judaea's summer camps.

30

A Tree Grove in Oz

ח-ר-שׁ

het-resh-shin

Family harmony often depends on a tacit agreement to forgo finicky fault finding. Amos Oz, in *A Tale of Love and Darkness* (Harvest Books), describes a pleasant Tu Bishvat outing with his often-discordant parents to a חוּרְשָׁה (*hursha*), a grove of trees, in suburban Jerusalem. When his usually pedantic father begins to expound fancifully on words associated with the root ח-ר-שׁ (*het, resh, shin*), his usually depressed mother whimsically adds her own list of derivations. Neither feels the need to tweak the other as they normally do, sensing, Oz implies, that creating associations among Hebrew words is a way of forging human links. Interestingly, no scholar has definitively pinpointed the source of the word *hursha* in relation to its root's other meanings. Today, we recognize the word mainly from Naomi Shemer's lilting song חֹרְשַׁת הָאֵיקָלִיפְטוּס (*horshat ha-ekaliptus*), "The Eucalyptus Grove."

Another meaning of the root *het-resh-shin* is to plow. This sense is found in the biblical prohibition in Deuteronomy לֹא תַחֲרֹשׁ (*lo taharosh*), "You shall not plow [using an ox and an ass together]." Samson uses the root metaphorically when he tells the Philistines they would never have gotten the answer to his riddle לוּלֵא חֲרַשְׁתֶּם בְּעֶגְלָתִי (*lulei harashtem be-eglati*), "had you not plowed with my heifer," i.e., plotted with Delilah to cajole the answer out of me.

In modern Hebrew, one finds מַחֲרֵשָׁה (*maharesha*), plow, and בֵּית חֲרוֹשֶׁת (*beit haroshet*), factory. Colloquially, the verb is used to describe long, arduous tasks, as when a student cramming for an exam חוֹרֵשׁ אֶת הַחֹומֶר (*horesh et ha-homer*), studies the material intensively, or an apartment seeker חוֹרֵשׁ אֶת הָעִיר (*horesh et ha-ir*), combs the entire city.

A different use of the root is found in the verbs חָרַשׁ (*harash*) and הֶחֱרִישׁ (*heherish*), to be silent, and, in the latter case, also to deafen by being loud. Related are the adverb חֶרֶשׁ (*heresh*), secretly; the adjective חֵרֵשׁ (*heresh*), deaf; and the doublet חֶרֶשׁ חֶרֶשׁ (*heresh heresh*), very quietly. Queen Esther explains to the Persian king that if Haman had not been bent on the utter destruction of the Jewish people, הֶחֱרַשְׁתִּי (*heherashti*), "I would have remained silent." The biblical injunction לֹא תְקַלֵּל חֵרֵשׁ (*lote-kallel heresh*), "Do not curse the deaf," is starkly ethical.

Some scholars want to find a connection between plowed land and a defective auditory canal. Amos Oz's parents found, with their selective deafness, in the woods and in words, a moment of family peace.

31

Labor and the Law

ט-ע-נ

tet-ayin-nun

You can never tell how many uses a two-trick pony will end up having. Take the example of ט–ע–נ (*tet, ayin, nun*), to load, to pierce. While the root appears only twice in Scripture, it has dozens of applications today.

In the story of Joseph and his brothers, Pharaoh, delighted to learn of the existence of his vizier Joseph's father, uses the root to instruct Joseph's brothers to טַעֲנוּ אֶת בְּעִירְכֶם (*ta'anu et be'irkhem*), load up your beasts of burden, return to Canaan and convince your father to come live in Egypt. We have to wait until the "Song of Scorn" (in Isaiah 14) to find the root again, albeit in a different register. There, Isaiah invokes, Dante-like, a dead Babylonian king condemned to walk around the underworld among מְטֹעֲנֵי חָרֶב (*meto'anei harev*), "those pierced by a sword," or, more to our point, laden with a sword in the belly.

In the Talmud, legal-minded rabbis expanded the meaning of the biblical root by bringing it into Jewish law courts—especially in commercial cases when a טוֹעֵן (*to'en*), claimant, brings a suit against a נִטְעָן (*nit'an*), defendant, who admits only partial responsibility.

The Talmud adds an interpersonal ethical component when it asserts that מִצְוָה לִטְעוֹן (*mitsva lit'on*), one is obliged to help a neighbor load his goods. Yet, when a מַטְעִין דְּבָרָיו (*mat'in devarav*), traveling salesman, adds a load of slanderous gossip to the wares he peddles, he incurs the opprobrium of the rabbis. In a definite ethical advance, Israel, since the 1990s, has certified a טוֹעֶנֶת רַבָּנִית (*to'enet rabbanit*), female rabbinic advocate, to represent the female litigant in divorce or family court.

Today, the port of Tel Aviv is a leisure time hot spot. In the 1930s, poet Leah Goldberg used our root in what has become a rousing Zionist anthem to celebrate the newly built commercial port there—taking special pride in the constant flow of סִירוֹת מִטְעָן (*sirot mit'an*), cargo boats. In an army tank, a טָעָן (*ta'an*), loader of ammunition, is both the soldier and machine. Be careful handling a מִטְעָן חַבָּלָה (*mit'an habbalah*), explosive charge, a task for which great care is טָעוּן (*ta'un*), required. Tech users might want לִטְעוֹן (*lit'on*), to upload software or, using a מַטְעֵן (*mat'en*), charger, recharge one's cellphone battery.

If any readers have טָעֲנוֹת וּמַעֲנוֹת (*teanot u-ma'anot*), an argumentative "bone to pick," with this column, remember, sword-piercing is a trick the pony has by now forgotten.

32

Creative Add-Ons

ט-פ-ל

tet-feh-lamed

At first glance, tapeworms, your children's nanny, root canals and chicken giblets would seem to have little in common. In Hebrew, surprisingly, they are all tied to the three-letter root ט-פ-ל (*tet, feh, lamed*), to attach, plaster over. While it is relatively easy to see how the adjective טָפֵל (*tafel*), secondary, incidental, comes from our root—an add-on is by its nature subordinate—it takes some imagination to picture how the other meanings evolved.

In the Bible, both Job and the Psalmist use the root vituperatively. Job, for his part, accuses his consolers of calumny, not condolences, saying, אַתֶּם טֹפְלֵי שָׁקֶר (*atem toflei sheker*), "you plaster falsehood," or invent lies. According to one commentator, by covering him over with falsehood, Job's accusers make his true character unrecognizable. The Psalmist says his detractors טָפְלוּ עָלַי שָׁקֶר (*taflu alai sheker*), "have accused me falsely." Recognizing the usefulness of a colorful idiom when he sees one, the author of the Yom Kippur *viddui* liturgy inserts the expression טָפַלְנוּ שָׁקֶר (*tafalnu sheker*), we have falsely accused others, in his litany of breast-beating confessions.

The rabbis of the Talmud use the root in Aramaic to take it in a different direction. They recognized that children are טְפוּלִין (*tefulin*), attached to, i.e., financially dependent on, their parents. The rabbis colorfully used טָפֵל (*tefel*), putty, as a generic term for children. Would it be going too far to speculate that, in the eyes of the rabbis, אֱמוּנוֹת טְפֵלוֹת (*emunot tefeilot*), superstitions, are childish by their very nature? Or are *emunot tefeilot* merely add-ons to our core beliefs?

Children and caregiving go together in many ways. From the infinitive לְטַפֵּל (*le-tappel*), to take care of, we have a מְטַפֶּלֶת (*metappelet*), nanny or babysitter. An Israeli might say of a person unusually sensitive to another, הוּא טִפֵּל בּוֹ בִּקְצוֹת הָאֶצְבָּעוֹת (*hu tippel bo bi-ketsot ha-etsba'ot*), he handled him with kid gloves, literally, with his fingertips. Speaking of highly sensitive things, our root also takes us to another kind of root, this one at the dentist's office, where טִפּוּל שֹׁרֶשׁ (*tippul shoresh*) is a root canal procedure. In biology, an organism that attaches itself to another and feeds off it is called a טַפִּיל (*tappil*), parasite—a tapeworm, or perhaps a twenty-something who won't move out of his parents' house.

Though our grandmother recognized that a chicken's breasts and thighs were primary, she also knew how to make good use of the טְפָלִים (*tiflayim*), giblets. Who says the secondary can't be made primary?

33

Treif Is as *Treif* Does

W hence do I love thee? Hebrew poet Yehuda Amichai
addresses this question as only a Jewish poet can. He finds
the source of his love in a single biblical verse taken from
the vast corpus of Jewish law regarding kashrut: forbidding the
seething of a baby goat in its mother's milk. Amichai's "In Place of
a Love Poem" talks about what we call in Yinglish today *treif*—a
synonym for unkosher—whose Hebrew root, ט-ר-פ (*tet, resh, feh*),
to tear to pieces, opens up a whole universe of human experience.

The root appears in Scripture in reference to טֹרְפֵי טָרֶף (*torfei
taref*), "ferocious beasts," i.e., those that tear their prey to pieces. It
is also used when human life goes terribly wrong. Job bitterly
blames God for his tragic fate, saying אַפּוֹ טָרַף (*apo taraf*), "In His
wrath He has torn me apart." When Joseph's brothers return from
the field with Joseph's tunic torn to pieces, their father, Jacob, cries
out טָרֹף טֹרַף יוֹסֵף (*tarof toraf Yosef*), "Joseph has surely been torn
limb from limb."

In gentler contexts, we praise the Woman of Valor when תִּתֵּן
טֶרֶף לְבֵיתָהּ (*titein teref le-veita*), "she provides sustenance for her
family." Certainly, *teref* cannot be forbidden meat, torn from live
animals. In this case, we learn, *teref* is simply a word for food in
general. In the story of Noah, we find our root in the mouth of the
dove who returns to the ark: וְהִנֵּה עֲלֵה זַיִת טָרָף בְּפִיהָ (*ve-hineh aleh
zayyit taraf be-fiy-hah*), "Behold a plucked-off olive leaf is in her
mouth."

In talmudic times, a rabbinic court could issue a טַרְפָּא (*tirpa*),
bill of seizure, allowing a lender to forcibly repossess his property.
The Mishna tells a fascinating story of Rabbi Tarfon, whose name
is a word for *kohen,* derived from the Greek. He plays Hebraically
on his name. It appears that as a judge, Rabbi Tarfon had mistakenly

acted as a טַרְפָן (*torfan*), someone who declares a kosher-slaughtered animal טָרֵף (*taref*), unkosher. Offering reimbursement, he mumbles to himself הָלְכָה הַמּוֹרְךָ, טַרפוֹן (*halkhah hamorkha, tarfon*), "You *torfan* you, you will now have to pay with your donkey for your mistake." Rabbi Tarfon's muttering lives on today as a contemporary Hebrew proverb for error-prone experts.

   Each new morning, you might want to rip off a page from your לוּחַ טָרָף (*lu'ah taraf*), page-a-day calendar. Crack an egg and beat it vigorously to cook a בֵּיצָה טְרוּפָה (*beitsah terufah*), scrambled egg. At the card table, players take turns לִטְרוֹף (*litrof*), to shuffle the deck. And, if you are a poet madly in love, you can easily become מְטֹרָף (*metoraf*), discombobulated, imagining seething goats everywhere.

34

All Together Now, Individually

י-ח-ד

yod-het-dalet

According to language scholar Frederick Greenspan, there are 289 absolute *hapax legomena* in the Hebrew bible—יְחִידָאִים (*yehida'im*), words that appear only once in Scripture. Among these are such common words as אֱגוֹז (*egoz*), nut, and גְּבִינָה (*gevina*), cheese. Ironically, the root from which *yehida'i* derives, י-ח-ד (*yod, het, dalet*), meaning both individually and together, is found abundantly in both Jewish sources and secular settings.

In Genesis, God tells Abraham to take יְחִידְךָ (*yehidekha*), "your only son," to offer as a sacrifice. Does Isaac acquiesce? From the verse וַיֵּלְכוּ שְׁנֵיהֶם יַחְדָּו (*va-yelkhu sheneihem yahdav*), "they went together," commentators assert that father and son are of one mind. Offered the Torah at Mount Sinai, the Israelites answer יַחְדָּו (*yahdav*), in unison, "We will do it." The psalmist provides the lyrics for a popular communal song: "How pleasant it is, שֶׁבֶת אַחִים גַּם יָחַד (*shevet ahim gam yahad*), for brothers to assemble together." He also has something to say about today's affairs of state, identifying Jerusalem as עִיר שֶׁחֻבְּרָה לָּהּ יַחְדָּו (*ir she-hubra la yahdav*), a city knit together. Medieval linguist David Kirnhi says that in the mouth of King David, the word יְחִידָתִי (*yehidati*), my oneness, implicitly means "my soul."

Then there is Judaism's contribution to civilization, אֱמוּנַת הַיִּחוּד (*emunat ha-yihud*), monotheism. Maimonides's *Guide for the Perplexed* describes Jews as הַמְיַחֲדִים (*ha-meyahadim*), those who truly proclaim God's oneness. In Solomon Alkabetz's *Lekha Dodi* hymn, God is called אֵל הַמְיֻוחָד (*el ha-meyuhad*), the one and only God. The Mishna tells us that the first man was created יְחִידִי (*yehidi*), alone, to teach that he who destroys a single life destroys an entire world.

Our root can be found throughout contemporary Hebrew, from the grammatical term לְשׁוֹן יָחִיד (*leshon yahid*), singular, to יְחִידָה (*yehida*), a unit, of the army or of a textbook. The expression בֵּן יָחִיד (*ben yahid*), only son, is sometimes used pejoratively to refer to a spoiled brat. We know that there are יְחִידִים (*yehidim*), a few individuals, who don't agree with the majority. Both saints and soldiers often pray בְּהִתְיַחֲדוּת (*be-hityahadut*), in solitude. We admire יְחִידֵי סְגוּלָה (*yehidei segula*), elite individuals, just as we respect רְשׁוּת הַיָּחִיד (*reshut ha-yahid*), private property.

In this column יִחַדְנוּ בְּיַחַד אֶת הַדִּבּוּר (*yihadnu be-yahad et ha-dibbur*), we have together focused on *yahad* and *yahid*. But let us not forget that there are other words, יְחִידִים בְּמִינָם (*yehidim be-minam*), one of a kind, that embellish the Hebrew language, even as they give us cheese and nuts to chew on.

35

Take My Advice ... Please

י-ע-צ

yod-ayin-tsadi

What do an attorney general, a school psychologist, a cosmetologist and Jacob J. Lew have in common? Give or take a few cultural nuances, they are all associated with the Hebrew root י-ע-צ (*yod, ayin, tsadi*), to advise. The root runs through several stories of intrigue at King David's court. During the clash between David and his son Absalom, Ahitophel, the king's יוֹעֵץ (*yo'ets*), adviser, commits treason by giving sound military advice to rebellious Absalom. What emerges when the advice is not followed is not only Ahitophel's suicide and Absalom's defeat and death, but also a modern Hebrew idiom, עֲצַת אֲחִיתֹפֶל (*atsat ahitophel*), ironically, bad advice. Later, the prophet Nathan whispers to Bathsheba אִיעָצֵךְ נָא עֵצָה (*i'atsekh na etsah*), "Let me give you a piece of advice," counseling her to deceive the aged king into naming her son, Solomon, king. Do not confuse פֶּלֶא יוֹעֵץ (*pele yo'ets*), Isaiah's designation for an ideal ruler, with יוֹעֵץ פֶּלֶא (*yo'ets pele*), modern slang for a giver of mind-boggling advice.

The midrash on the book of Esther tells a sweet tale using our root. Mordecai would go about the city of Shushan asking Jewish children to recite a biblical verse. When one lad quotes Isaiah's prophecy, עֻצוּ עֵצָה וְתֻפָר (*utsu etsah ve-tu-far*), "Conspire conspiracies all you wish, they will come to naught," Mordecai's resolve to defeat Haman is strengthened. *Pirke Avot* teaches that 50 is the גִּיל הָעֵצָה (*gil ha-etsah*), age of wisdom. Nevertheless, the Talmud hints that we can also seek wisdom from nephrologists; after all, according to tractate Berakhot, כְּלָיוֹת יוֹעֲצוֹת (*kelayot yo'atsot*), "The kidneys are the seat of guidance."

Lew, as chief of staff and then treasury secretary to President Obama, was what Jewish communities in earlier times called a יוֹעֵץ סְתָרִים (*yo'ets setarim*), confidential adviser. A recent development in synagogue life is the יוֹעֶצֶת הֲלָכָה (*yo'etset halakhah*), adviser on sensitive women's health issues and Jewish law. In Israeli schools, the יוֹעֶצֶת חִינּוּכִית (*yo'etset hinukhit*), educational consultant, often deals with psychological problems on site, while a יוֹעֶצֶת יוֹפִי (*yo'etset yofi*), beauty consultant, helps customers choose appropriate cosmetics. Not unlike an attorney general, Israel's יוֹעֵץ הַמִּשְׁפָּטִי לָמֶמְשָׁלָה (*yo'ets ha-mish-pati la-memshala*), governmental legal counsel, has prosecutorial powers.

The word מוֹעֵצָה (*mo'atsah*)—in English, council; in Russian, *soviet*—gives us מוֹעֶצֶת הַבִּטָּחוֹן (*mo'etset ha-bitahon*), security council, and בְּרִית הַמּוֹעֲצוֹת (*berit ha-mo'atsot*), Soviet Union. A silver-tongued negotiator might offer לְכָה וְנִנָּעֲצָה יַחְדָּו (*lekha ve-niva'atsah, yahdav*), "Come, let us reason together." But be נוֹעֵץ (*no'ats*), advised: flowery phrases often conceal hidden agendas.

36

Thou Shalt Be Creative

י-צ-ר

yod-tsadi-resh

A yeshiva student who is a houseguest emerges somewhat sheepishly from the lavatory and addresses a request for toilet tissue to his hostess: "May I have some אֲשֶׁר יָצַר (*asher yatsar*) paper, please?" This humorous euphemism is a creative allusion to what is known as the *Asher Yatsar* blessing—"Who has formed human beings [with wisdom]"—recited on completing a bodily function. The Hebrew root from which this blessing derives, י-צ-ר (*yod, tsadi, resh*), to create, to produce, tells many other stories as well.

In Scripture, God, the יוֹצֵר אוֹר (*yotser or*), Creator of light, asserts that Israel is עַם זוּ יָצַרְתִּי לִי (*am zu yatsarti li*), "the people I have created for myself." Our sages, reading Genesis 2:7, noticed that the verb וַיִּיצֶר (*va-yitser*), "[God] formed [man]," is spelled with a double *yod*. From this seeming superfluity they create a whole philosophy of life. The two *yods*, they propose, suggest that man was created with two *yetsers*, יֵצֶר הַטּוֹב (*yetser ha-tov*), the good inclination, and יֵצֶר הָרָע (*yetser ha-ra*), the evil inclination. They conclude that human beings have free will to choose between these two natural dispositions and are therefore responsible for their actions. Significantly, in Genesis 2:19, when the animal kingdom is created, וַיִּצֶר (*va-yitser*) has only one *yod*.

The rabbis of *Pirke Avot* give the root a subtle meaning, answering the question "Who is strong?" with הַכּוֹבֵשׁ אֶת יִצְרוֹ (*ha-kovesh et yitsro*), "One who conquers his will." We are also reminded that were it not for what we call יֵצֶר הַמִּין (*yetser ha-min*), the libido, no one would propagate the species. The Talmud uses our root creatively to express Jewish guilt, in the saying אוֹי לִי מִיּוֹצְרִי וְאוֹי לִי מִיִּצְרִי (*oy li mi-yotsri ve-oy li mi-yitsri*), My Creator punishes my evil doings and my conscience punishes my evil thoughts.

Many Jews, whether they live here or there, will go out of their way to buy תּוֹצֶרֶת הָאָרֶץ (*totseret ha-arets*), goods produced in Israel. Look at the label of any local מוּצָר (*mutsar*), product, and you will see the indication, מְיוּצָר עַל יְדֵי (*meyutsar al yedei*), manufactured by. Immigrants to Israel would often marvel at their new language. Take for example the following overheard conversation: "In the old country, he was a poor *schnaider*, tailor; here in Israel he's already a יַצְרָן (*yatsran*), manufacturer."

When someone asks why you chose your line of work, if you are יְצִירָתִי (*yetsirati*), creative, you can answer, לְכָךְ נוֹצָרְתִּי (*le-khakh notsarti*), that's what I was created for—an answer appropriate for Hebrew columnists, and for yeshiva students as well.

37

Sitting on the Hebrew Fence

י-שִׁ-ב

yod-shin-vet

We all know about Balaam's ass, the talking donkey that berates its master, but what of Abraham's donkey in the biblical story of the Sacrifice of Isaac? We encounter the donkey in Abraham's command to his servants, שְׁבוּ לָכֶם פֹּה עִם הַחֲמוֹר (*shevu lakhem po im ha-hamor*), "Sit here with the donkey." The donkey's job is ostensibly לָשֶׁבֶת (*la-shevet*), to "hang around," while Abraham takes his son Isaac up to Mount Moriah. The midrash suggests that the donkey underscores the servants' indifference to the extraordinary nearby event. The Hebrew language, for its part, makes much of the root י-שׁ-ב (*yod, shin, vet*), to sit, inhabit, populate.

The root appears some 800 times in Scripture. An aged Abraham יֹשֵׁב פֶּתַח הָאֹהֶל (*yoshev petah ha-ohel*), "is sitting at his tent's entrance," when angels arrive to announce his future paternity. After 40 years of wandering, the Israelites enter Canaan, אֶרֶץ נוֹשָׁבֶת (*eretz noshavet*), "a populated land." On Tisha B'Av, we lament that formerly densely populated Jerusalem after the destruction of the Temple is יָשְׁבָה בָדָד (*yashva vadad*), dwelling in solitude. In the prestate יִשׁוּב (*yishuv*), settlement, of Palestine, soldiers of the Palmach used another psalm while sitting around the campfire, singing, "How good and pleasant it is," שֶׁבֶת אַחִים גַּם יָחַד (*shevet ahim gam yahad*), "for brothers to sit together."

Biblical judge Deborah יוֹשֶׁבֶת (*yoshevet*), sits in judgment, under her palm tree, while rabbinic Hebrew uses the infinitive לֵישֵׁב (*leishev*) in connection with court proceedings. Rashi, the great Torah commentator, asserts that his function is לְיַשֵׁב פְּשׁוּטוֹ שֶׁל מִקְרָא (*le-yashev peshuto shel mikra*), "to provide a solid 'seat' on which to base the plain meaning of the biblical text."

Israeli songwriter Arik Einstein sings of an indecisive friend who יוֹשֵׁב עַל הַגָּדֵר (*yoshev al ha-gader*), "straddles the fence." In today's Hebrew, a מוֹשָׁב (*moshav*) can refer to a cooperative settlement, a car seat, a home for the aged or even the Russian Pale of Settlement. In addition, יְשִׁיבָה (*yeshivah*) can allude to the sitting position, a business or political meeting or a talmudic academy. And what about both sides of יַשְׁבָן (*yashvan*)? According to the word's coiner, journalist Itamar Ben-Avi, son of Eliezer Ben-Yehuda, the reviver of the Hebrew language, it denotes a "colonizer." For the rest of us, it's the part of our body we sit on. Whether we talk or remain silent depends on how much יִשּׁוּב הַדַּעַת (*yishuv ha-da'at*), peace of mind, we have.

38

Help Wanted

י-שׁ-ע

yod-shin-ayin

At Hanukka we light many candles and we cook with plenty of oil. To commemorate the liberation of the Temple linguistically, we say—from the root י-שׁ-ע (*yod, shin, ayin*)—several variations of a Hebrew word for deliverance. Originally, this root meant to be capacious. It probably took several linguistic leaps to take us from wide open spaces to sufficiency to a sense of liberation. Some scholars conjecture that there might have been a secondary root, שׁ-ו-ע (*shin, vav, ayin*), but that root probably merits its own treatment. We find our root at Hanukka time in the hymn *Ma'oz Tzu*, יְשׁוּעָתִי (*yeshu'ati*), Mighty Rock of "my salvation," and in a prayer appended to the *Amida*, where God is praised for the תְּשׁוּעוֹת (*teshu'ot*), salvations, of Hanukka and Purim.

The root is found prominently in uses of הוֹשַׁע נָא (*hosha na*) in the Hallel service, a verb meaning "Save, I pray." On Sukkot, הוֹשַׁעֲנוֹת (*hoshanot*) are willow branches that are beaten on הוֹשַׁעֲנָא רַבָּה (*hoshana rabba*), the seventh day of the holiday. A הוֹשַׁעֲנָא חֲבוּטָה (*hoshana havuta*), beaten willow, is an expression that can be used to denote any useless thing and, by extension, also a person who is good for nothing. The expression חֲסַר יֶשַׁע (*hasar yesha*), helpless, does not have the same critical connotation.

The names of many biblical figures derive from our root, including יְשַׁעְיָהוּ (*yeshayahu*), Isaiah, the sublime prophet, and Moses' successor הוֹשֵׁעַ (*hoshe'a*), Hosea, before he became יְהוֹשֻׁעַ (*yehoshu'a*), Joshua.

In Christianity, a Hosanna is often a song of praise, especially when sung by Harry Belafonte on his *Calypso* album. Salvation is a quasi-military term, particularly in the Hebrew חֵיל הַיֶּשַׁע (*heil ha-yesha*), Salvation Army. While Judaism applies the word מוֹשִׁיעַ (*moshi'a*), savior, to God alone, it is no surprise that our root also appears in the name יֵשׁוּעַ (*yeshu'a*), Jesus, and in the sect founded by Ignatius Loyola, יְשׁוּעִים (*yeshu'im*), Jesuits. These names are not to be confused with the יֵשׁוּעַ הַבֵּן (*yeshu'a ha-ben*), saving of the son, a talmudic term for the Jewish custom—more commonly known by the Yiddish *vakhnakht*—of reciting the Shema in the house of an infant to ward off evil spirits the evening before his circumcision.

The *havdala* service, recited at the end of Sabbath and holidays, begins with the invocation of the God of *yeshu'ati*, my salvation. Before drinking the wine, we raise כּוֹס יְשׁוּעוֹת (*kos yeshu'ot*), a cup connoting saving acts.

What is special here is that, from latkes to lights to libations, one finds the language of salvation everywhere.

39

Much Ado About More

י-ת-ר

yod-tav-resh

Is it possible that Moses married for money? After all, his father-in-law was יִתְרוֹ (*yitro*), Jethro. This name derives from the root י-ת-ר (*yod, tav, resh*), rich and abundant. The Rabbis, however, argued that he was called Yitro because he did abundant good deeds or, alternatively, because he had an abundance of names. In addition, a form of our root means both to bind and to stretch; this explains the existence of יֶתֶר (*yeter*), tendon, which attaches the muscle to the bone, and כְּלֵי מֵיתָר (*kelei meitar*), string instruments, whose cords one stretches tight.

The root is found in abundance in Scripture in an abundance of contexts. Forefather Jacob gives his son Reuven the blessing יֶתֶר שְׂאֵת וְיֶתֶר עָז (*yeter se'et ve-yeter oz*), abundant vigor and power. Scripture, referring to sacrifices, speaks of the יֹתֶרֶת עַל הַכָּבֵד (*yoteret al ha-kaved*), a membrane appended to the animal's liver. Leftovers were not a biblical custom. Eating the paschal lamb, the Israelites were told לֹא תוֹתִירוּ מִמֶּנּוּ עַד בֹּקֶר (*lo totiru mimenu ad boker*), "You shall not leave any of it over till morning." Yet, a miracle performed by the prophet Elisha involved a small quantity of ingredients providing אָכֹל וְהוֹתֵר (*ekhol ve-hoter*), enough food to eat and leave over. Isaiah proclaimed that if God had not הוֹתִיר לָנוּ שָׂרִיד כִּמְעַט (*hotir lanu sarid kime'at*), "left us a small remnant," we would have disappeared from the face of the earth. The preacher of Ecclesiastes stresses that מוֹתַר הָאָדָם (*motar ha-adam*), "man's advantage" over animals is nil.

Moving to modern times, in place of Google's "I'm feeling lucky" button, the Hebrew version of the company's home page jokingly has יוֹתֵר מַזָּל מִשֵּׂכֶל (*yoter mazal mi-sekhel*), "more luck than brains." A sports announcer will inform listeners which side has the יִתְרוֹן (*yitron*), lead. Furthermore, יֶתֶר עַל כֵּן (*yeter al ken*), the plural

יִתְרוֹנוֹת (*yitronot*), applies to one's advantages, while מוֹתָרוֹת (*motarot*) refers to luxuries one permits oneself. Inter alia, בֵּין הַיֶּתֶר (*bein ha-yeter*), the word יֶתֶר (*yeter*) is used for both an archer's bowstring and the hypotenuse of a right triangle. All these homonyms are enough to give one יֶתֶר לַחַץ (*yeter lahats*), hypertension.

Proper decorum teaches that one should not insist יוֹתֵר מִדַּי (*yoter mi-dai*), too much, on one's rights; rather, one should be willing at times לְוַתֵּר (*le-vater*), to relinquish them. On Friday eve, however, one need not forsake the blessing of נְשָׁמָה יְתֵרָה (*neshama yetera*), extra soul, the spiritual elation that accompanies the Jewish people on the Sabbath. Certainly, neither Moses nor his father-in-law could have found this extra soul מְיֻתָּר (*meyutar*), superfluous.

Heavy Lifting

כ-ב-ד
khof-vet-dalet

Have you ever wondered why the commandment כַּבֵּד אֶת אָבִיךָ
וְאֵת אִמֶּךָ (*kabbed et avikha ve-et immekha*), "Honor your
father and mother," is placed right next to the commandment
to observe the Sabbath? According to Jewish feminist pioneer Blu
Greenberg, it's a matter of timing. Just as the Sabbath arrives
whether one is ready or not, so, too, even though the duty of caring
for aged parents may come at an inopportune time, one must take up
the burden whenever it presents itself. The root כ-ב-ד (*khof, vet,
dalet*) is heavy with meanings, including—besides honor—
weightiness and sweeping.

In Scripture, a dozen words, some carrying several
meanings, are derived from the root. Our forefather Abram is כָּבֵד
בַּמִּקְנֶה (*kaved ba-mikneh*), "a wealthy cattleman." Jacob's eyes, we
learn, כָּבְדוּ מִזֹּקֶן (*kavdu mi-zoken*), "became dim from age." In the
Exodus story, the verb לְהַכְבִּיד (*le-hakhbid*) describes God's
hardening of Pharaoh's heart. When God orders Moses to speak with
Pharaoh, the Israelite leader begs off with the excuse of being כְּבַד
פֶּה (*kevad peh*), "heavy mouthed," with a speech impediment. Psalm
45, a love song honoring a king and his "princess bride," has an
enigmatic metaphorical expression, כָּל כְּבֻדָּה בַת מֶלֶךְ פְּנִימָה (*kol
kevuddah vat melekh penimah*), "the treasures of a princess are
inside." In some religious circles, this suggests that Jewish girls, for
their honor, should not mingle in the public sphere. El Al, the Israeli
airline, alerts passengers to a more concrete issue, כְּבוּדָה מוּתֶּרֶת
(*kevudah muteret*), baggage allowance. In rabbinic literature, it is
considered bad form לְהִתְכַּבֵּד (*le-hitkabed*), to exalt oneself over
others.

Today, to let your neighbor get out of the elevator before
you, just bow your head slightly and say בְּכָבוֹד (*be-khavod*), after

you. Prior to a lecture, a כִּבּוּד קַל (*kibbud kal*), light refreshment—in Hebrew it reads like an oxymoron—is often served. Circulating with a מְכַבֶּדֶת (*mekhabeddet*), serving tray, the hostess announces הִתְכַּבְּדוּ מְכֻבָּדִים (*hitkabdu mekhubadim*), "Honored guests, please partake!" After the festivities—perhaps to make the room look respectable again?—a כַּבְדָן (*kabdan*), sweeper, comes by with a מַכְבֵּדֶת (*makhbeddet*), broom, to clean up.

A neurologist may be concerned with a patient's מֶרְכַּז הַכֹּבֶד (*merkaz ha-koved*), center of gravity, while a nuclear scientist in Dimona experiments בְּכֹבֶד רֹאשׁ (*be-khoved rosh*), serious-mindedly, with מַיִם כְּבֵדִים (*mayim keveidim*), heavy water.

Finally, to those who make time to study Hebrew, this chapter declares כָּל הַכָּבוֹד (*kol ha-kavod*), all honor to you!

41

The Container and the Contained

כ-ו-ל
khof-vav-lamed

In Israel, when your shopping list is too short for a trip to the supermarket, head for the corner מַכּוֹלֶת (*makolet*), grocery. In the Bible, *makolet* means simply food, shortened from מַאֲכוֹלֶת (*ma'akholet*), from the root א-כ-ל (*alef, khof, lamed*), to eat. Medieval linguist David Kimchi (Radak), however, relates that his father would derive *makolet* from the verb לְהָכִיל (*le-hakhil*), to contain, using the root כ-ו-ל (*khof, vav, lamed*), to include, contain, measure, sustain, endure. Many view a *makolet* as a small market that "contains" a profusion of provisions.

Isaiah, in a threnody of consolation, emphasizes God's power over the infinite: וְכָל (*ve-khal*), "[He] measures" the dust of the earth. The prophet Amos is told by an antagonistic priest that the land itself will not be able לְהָכִיל (*le-hakhil*), to endure, his prophecies. Jeremiah calls the residents of Judah broken cisterns that לֹא יָכְלוּ הַמַּיִם (*lo yakhlu ha-mayim*), "could not hold water," telling them to repent of having served false gods.

Genesis, doubling the root, asserts that Joseph, in charge of food rations in Egypt, was kindhearted toward his kin: וַיְכַלְכֵּל יוֹסֵף (*va-yekhalkel yosef*), "Joseph sustained with food [his father and brothers]." We know that legal papers are supposed to be brief from Radak, who interprets the psalmist's יְכַלְכֵּל דְּבָרָיו בְּמִשְׁפָּט (*yekhalkel devarav be-mishpat*): "God measures out his judgments not only equably but also succinctly." From this measuring we get the modern science of כַּלְכָּלָה (*kalkala*), economics.

The authors of the Siddur inserted the phrase מְכַלְכֵּל חַיִּים בְּחֶסֶד (*mekhalkel hayyim be-hesed*), "God measures out life with kindness," into the *Amidah* prayer. Two midrashic treatments of Exodus, attributed to Rabbis Yishmael and Simon ben Yohai, are called מְכִילְתָּא (*mekhilta*), collection of interpretations.

Several modern words are drawn from the root. A shipment of oil or gas may be transported in a מְכָלִית (*mekhalit*), tanker. On making *aliya*, one may ship one's household goods to Israel in a מְכוּלָה (*mekhulah*), container (more commonly a "lift"—even in Hebrew). The expression תְּכוּלַת הַבַּיִת (*tekhulat ha-bayit*) designates the contents of a house. During the recent catastrophe in Japan, many a house was destroyed in עַל תְּכוּלָתוֹ (*al tekhulato*), in its entirety.

One may need the intellectual flexibility of Radak's father to derive from our root, as some do, several similar-looking words: תַּכְלִית (*takhlit*), purpose; כּוֹלֵל (*kolel*), yeshiva for married men; כִּילִי (*kili*), tightwad; כַּיָּל (*kayyal*), surveyor; מִכְלָלָה (*mikhlala*), college; or מִכְלָאָה (*mikhla'ah*), holding pen for prisoners.

Ponder these on your walk home from the *makolet*.

42

The Qualities of Quantity

כ-מ-ה
khof-mem-heh

What do Don Giovanni, Karl Marx and Ahad Ha-Am have in common? All three—whether for reasons of libido, economics or Zionist fervor—suggest that quantity is more important than quality. The root כ-מ-ה (*khof, mem, heh*), to quantify, offers several complexities. Some medieval grammarians hold that the basic root is מ-ה (*mem, heh*), as in Jacob's exclamation מָה נּוֹרָא (*ma nora*), "How wondrous [is this place]!" and Balaam's blessing, מַה טֹבוּ (*ma tovu*), "How goodly [are your tents, O Jacob]!"

In Genesis, Pharaoh asks Jacob, כַּמָּה יְמֵי שְׁנֵי חַיֶּיךָ (*kamma yemei shenei hayyekha*), "How many days are the years of your life?" Today we would ask, בֶּן כַּמָּה אַתָּה (*ben kamma ata*), how old are you?

The Babylonian Talmud records that Moses issued כַּמָּה תַּקָּנוֹת (*kamma takkanot*), several reforms. The Jerusalem Talmud suggests that שְׁמוֹנִים וְכַמָּה (*shemonim ve-khamma*), 80-plus, prophets inaugurated a certain prayer. Both Talmuds use the expression עַל אַחַת כַּמָּה וְכַמָּה (*al ahat kamma ve-khamma*), all the more so, to introduce the conclusion of *a fortiori* reasoning.

A 16th-century kabbalist, Eleazar ben Moses Azikri of Safed, proclaims in a love poem to God—"*Yedid Nefesh*," today in Israel-oriented synagogues tacked on to the front of the *Kabbalat Shabbat* service—כִּי זֶה כַּמָּה (*ki zeh kamma*), "For this is how much" I yearn to see God's glorious power.

From the sublime we go to the restaurant. When asking your waiter for the bill, you might wonder, כַּמָּה הַנֶּזֶק (*kamma ha-nezek*), what's the damage?

Speaking for the Hebrew Language Academy, linguist Ruth Almagor-Ramon asserts that because כַּמּוּת (*kammut*), quantity, is used to measure things that cannot be counted, like sand, or to count things with little individual worth, like buttons, it would be in bad taste to use *kammut* for counting people. At the wholesaler, therefore, you will want to know if you can get a product in כַּמּוּיוֹת גְדוֹלוֹת (*kammuyot gedolot*), large quantities, for the party to which you invited מִסְפַּר אֲנָשִׁים (*mispar anashim*), a number of people.

Stroll into the *shuk* and ask כַּמָּה זֶה עוֹלֶה (*kamma zeh oleh*), how much does this cost? Nowadays, עַד כַּמָּה שֶׁיָּדוּעַ לָנוּ (*ad kamma she-yadu'a lanu*), as far as we know, you will get the answer, רק כַּמָּה שְׁקָלִים (*rak kamma shekalim*), just a few shekels. If you think that is too much, tell the merchant you'll be back in כַּמָּה יָמִים (*kamma yamim*), a few days. That way, in addition to a quantity of money, you will be able to spend some quality time in Israel.

43

In Good Company

ל-ו-ה

lamed-vav-heh

What do Sputnik, the Desert Tabernacle, the Bank of Israel, Jewish funerals and the sea monster-that-became-God's-playmate have to do with each other? They are all related to the Hebrew root ל-ו-ה (*lamed, vav, heh*), to accompany, connect.

In Genesis, Leah, sensing that her husband, Jacob, has withdrawn from her emotionally, uses our root to name her third son לֵוִי (*levi*), Levi. She explains her choice both psychologically and etymologically, lamenting, יִלָּוֶה אִישִׁי אֵלַי (*yilaveh ishi eilai*), "may my husband [now] draw closer to me." One can find corroboration of Leah's linguistic fancy in the role the Levite tribe plays in the tabernacle ritual—as לְוִיִּם (*leviim*), adjuncts, to the *kohanim*, priests, who run the show. The book of Esther, in a magnificent gesture, enjoins not only the Jews but also כָּל הַנִּלְוִים עֲלֵיהֶם (*kol ha-nilvim aleihem*), all the non-Jews who have joined them, to celebrate Purim.

And what of the marvelous leviathan? We are free to conjecture this creature's outlandish function from a verse in picturesque Psalm 104, לִוְיָתָן זֶה יָצַרְתָּ לְשַׂחֶק בּוֹ (*livyatan zeh yatsarta le-sahek bo*), "You have created this leviathan to play with." It appears from this verse that God has created the sea creature as a companion for Himself.

Opinions are divided on whether לִוָּה (*livah*), to escort, and לָוָה (*lavah*), to borrow, are etymologically connected. One ingenious lexicographer, drawing on a phrase in Proverbs 22:7, עֶבֶד לוֶֹה לְאִישׁ מַלְוֶה (*eved loveh le-ish malveh*), "the borrower is slave to the lender," suggests that borrowers and lenders are joined by their הַלְוָאָה (*halva'ah*), debt, in common.

Do not confuse *halva'ah*, loan, with הַלְוָיָה (*halvayah*), funeral procession. What is commonly called in "Yinglish" a *levaya* has nothing to do with ceremonies at a funeral parlor. As the word's origin tells us, it is all about physically accompanying the deceased on his or her way to a final resting place. More cheerfully, the traditional "fourth Sabbath meal," the מְלַוֶּה מַלְכָּה (*melaveh malkah*), is our way of escorting the Sabbath Queen from the sacred Sabbath to the workaday week.

So where does Sputnik come in? Well, in Russian, the word sputnik means traveling companion; in scientific Hebrew, it's a לַוְיָן (*lavyan*), satellite.

Let's hope, הַלְוַאי (*halevai*), that one of the תּוֹפָעוֹת לְוַאי (*tofa'ot levai*), side benefits, of this chapter is בְּנֵי לְוָיָה (*bene levayah*), companions to travel with, Hebraically.

44

What's Old Is New

ל-ו-נ
lamed-vav-nun

ebrew is an "old-new" language. Its poetry derives from its lilting biblical archaisms and shiny neologisms. Take, for example, the root ל-ו-נ (*lamed, vav, nun*), to stay for the night. Because the root's meaning is circumscribed to a particular time—nighttime—scholars have conjectured that it is itself derived from yet another root, one that has its source in the word לַיְלָה (*layla*), night.

Even the root's restrictive meaning can be nuanced. In Jeremiah, a natural disaster leads some doubters to compare an absent God to an אֹרֵחַ נָטָה לָלוּן (*ore'ah natah la-lun*), "a traveler who stops for one night." In his 1996 novel of the same Hebrew name, *A Guest for the Night*, Nobel Prize laureate S.Y. Agnon adapts the biblical phrase to describe a traveler who can't bring himself to leave.

Using our root in an ethical context, Leviticus reminds employers of the duty to avoid הָלָנַת שָׂכָר (*halanat sakhar*), keeping a worker's wages overnight.

Several biblical uses of the root have to do with travel. Journeying from Moab to Bethlehem, Ruth pledges her loyalty to her mother-in-law, Naomi, saying בַּאֲשֶׁר תָּלִינִי אָלִין (*ba-asher talini alin*), "Where you lodge I will lodge."

On the road during his quest for a wife, Jacob finds some stones suitable for pillows, וַיָּלֶן שָׁם (*va-yalen sham*), and "stops for the night." Traveling back to Canaan with provisions they have bought in Egypt, Joseph's brothers stop at a מָלוֹן (*malon*), "night encampment," and are startled to find their knapsacks filled with money. Today, *malon* is a hotel; מְלוֹנַאי (*melonai*), hotelkeeper; and מְלוֹנִית (*melonit*), motel. Isaiah describes a מְלוּנָה (*melunah*) as a prototypical sukkah in which a watchman guarding the crops in the field would spend the night. Today, *melunah* is a dog kennel.

The Talmud offers an intriguing pitfall for misreading a phrase. The expression מַיִם שֶׁלָּנוּ (*mayim shellanu*) sounds like "our water." In the tractate that deals with baking *matzot* for Passover, however, the phrase refers to "water that has been kept overnight," in vessels protecting it from leaven.

When Hebrew national poet Hayyim Nahman Bialik, in his piece "My Poetry," addresses the question of the mournful sources of his writings, he uses our root to assert that it comes from a plaintive cricket that would מִתְלוֹנֵן (*mitlonen*), dwell, in the walls of his decrepit childhood home. Is Bialik playing with us here? Or is it only a linguistic coincidence that the noun תְּלוּנָה (*telunah*), complaint—a staple of his poetry—is derived from a different root that looks exactly like ours? What's old is often new, and vice versa.

45

No Xanax, Thanks; We're Israeli

ל-ח-צ
lamed-het-tsadi

According to some observers of the Israeli scene, there is one basic condition that characterizes its Jewish population: to be constantly בְּלַחַץ (*be-lahats*), under pressure. Israeli singer Kobi Oz protests frenetically and unconvincingly אֲנִי לֹא בְּלַחַץ (*ani lo be-lahats*), "I'm not stressed!" Others ask מָה הַלַּחַץ? (*ma ha-lahats*), What's the hurry?

Our root, ל-ח-צ (*lamed, het, tsadi*), to squeeze, to oppress, goes back to the Israelites' conditions in Egypt. In Exodus, God tells Moses that He has seen הַלַּחַץ אֲשֶׁר מִצְרַיִם לֹחֲצִים אֹתָם (*ha-lahats asher mitsrayim lohatsim otam*), "the oppression with which the Egyptians oppress them." In a verse recited at the Seder, we explain our liberation similarly: וַיַּרְא אֶת לַחֲצֵנוּ (*va-yar et lahatsenu*), "He saw our oppression."

Sometimes, talking donkeys use *lahats* in God's service. That's what comes from the story of Balaam's ass who, carrying his master to curse the Israelites, is blocked by an angel in a narrow pass. The story relates, וַתִּלָּחֵץ (*va-tilahets*), "[the ass] squeezed herself" against the wall and וַתִּלְחַץ (*va-tilhats*), "chafed" Balaam's leg painfully against it. Had Balaam been further penalized, he might have received other biblical punishments derived from our root: מַיִם לַחַץ (*mayim lahats*) and לֶחֶם לַחַץ (*lehem lahats*), the scanty amount of bread and water one is fed in prison.

The Talmud, in tractate Kiddushin, uses the root to make an ethical point about the treatment of a female prisoner of war: לֹא יְלָחֲצֶנָּה (*lo yilhatsena*), the capturing soldier "may not pressure her" to yield to him during the war.

Remember the days when couples danced while holding each other tightly in their arms? That type of slow dancing was called, with erotic connotations, רִקּוּד לַחַץ (*rikkud lahats*), a tight-hug dance. Today, a teenager in Israel, preparing for Army service, might use a לַחֲצִית (*lahatsit*), hand grip, for wrist-strengthening. A tailor, instead of attaching a button on a garment, can sew on a לְחָצָנִית (*lahtsanit*), snap fastener. A woodworker might make use of מֶלְחָצַיִם (*melhatsayim*), a vise. And let's not forget the politician running for office announcing that she is not לְחִיצָה (*lehitsa*), susceptible to pressure, from any קְבוּצַת לַחַץ (*kevutsat lahats*), pressure group. She is willing, however, לִלְחֹוץ יָדַיִם (*lilhots yadayim*), to shake hands, with all.

Many Israelis, who already live in a metaphorical סִיר לַחַץ (*sir lahats*), pressure cooker, lament that the American government לוֹחֶצֶת עָלֵינוּ (*lohetset aleinu*), puts pressure on us. No matter the situation, however, it is always advisable to try to control the level of one's לַחַץ דָּם (*lahats dam*), blood pressure.

46

Made to Measure

מ-ד-ד

mem-dalet-dalet

There are two types of people in this world: those who count and those who measure. The many ways Hebrew uses the root מ-ד-ד (*mem, dalet, dalet*), to measure (originally, to stretch out), are eminently countable. The original sense of the root is found in the biblical story of the prophet Elijah, telling how he brought a dead boy back to life: וַיִּתְמֹדֵד עַל הַיֶּלֶד (*va-yitmoded al ha-yeled*), "He stretched himself upon the child."

A measure of cloth can be sewn into a מַד (*mad*), garment. In the burnt-offering ceremony, the priest dons מִדּוֹ בַד (*middo bad*), his linen garment. In preparation for David's battle with Goliath, Saul offers him מַדָּיו (*maddav*), his own battle dress. In Judges, the song of Deborah relates that wealthy people would sit on מִדִּין (*middin*), saddle rugs, stretched over the backs of asses.

It appears that measurement was an obsession with the prophet Ezekiel, the visionary of the restored Temple, who uses our root more than 50 times. In measuring out the envisioned Temple, he uses an expression קְנֵה הַמִּדָּה, (*keneh ha-midda*), measuring reed, that flourishes in modern Hebrew with slightly different connotations—for example, a criterion or the scale on a map. Sometimes, a measure implies something large, as in Jeremiah's בֵּית מִדּוֹת (*beit middot*), big house, or in the 12 spies' depiction of Canaan's giants as אַנְשֵׁי מִדּוֹת (*anshei middot*), men of great stature.

The midrash warns against מִדַּת סְדֹם (*middat sedom*), Sodom-style measurement, where, reportedly, stretching human bodies or cutting off limbs made everyone fit into a one-size-fits-all bed. Opinions vary as to whether there are 7, 13 or 32 מִדּוֹת (*middot*), rules, for interpreting the Torah. The 13 *middot*, divine attributes of God, are chanted repeatedly on Yom Kippur.

These days, one is often asked לְהִתְמוֹדֵד עִם בְּעָיָה (*le-hitmoded im be'aya*), to deal with a problem, and to do so in a manner that is מִדּוֹתִי (*middoti*), ethical. Today's אִישׁ מִדּוֹת (*ish middot*), man of distinction, will have his suits made לְפִי מִדּוֹת (*le-fi middot*), to measure, except if he's in the army, where he will wear מַדִּים (*maddim*), an army uniform.

There are two types of Israeli drivers: those who resignedly pay the ticket for an expired מַדְחָן (*madhan*), parking meter, and those whose blood pressure rises on the מַדְלַחַץ (*madlahatz*), sphygmomanometer, the minute they get in the car. In either case, בְּמִדָּה מְסֻיֶּמֶת (*be-midda mesuyyemet*), to a certain extent, punishment is meted out מִדָּה כְּנֶגֶד מִדָּה (*midda ke-neged midda*), measure for measure.

47

Mixing Sense of It All

מ-ז-ג

mem-zayin-gimel

*Z*ionist wine lovers will certainly be pleased to hear that the biblical promise of "milk and honey" might be a metaphor for the white and red vintages that flow so abundantly in the modern State of Israel. Lovers of Hebrew will also enjoy the history behind a bizarre Hebrew root for wine, מ-ז-ג (*mem, zayin, gimel*), referring to a mixture of wine and water as well as to all types of blending.

The root appears in an erotic passage of the Song of Songs, in which the lover, comparing his beloved's belly to a rounded goblet, suddenly envisions the wine he would like to drink from that goblet. Ecstatically, he sings out, אַל יֶחְסַר הַמָּזֶג (*al yehsar ha-mazeg*), "Let there be no lack of [blended] wine!"

The root is found in abundance in rabbinic legal discussions. Too much water, say the rabbis, and the מְזוּג (*mizug*), mixture, is no longer considered wine for making a blessing. Too much wine in the mixture and, on Passover, you are too drunk to be counted as free from slavery. Wine שֶׁמְּזָגוֹ נָכְרִי (*she-mezago nokhri*), poured by an idol worshiper, is forbidden by rabbinic dictate. Naturally, Hillel and Shammai disagree whether מוֹזְגִין אֶת הַכּוֹס (*mozgin et ha-kos*), one pours the cup of wine, before or after washing the hands. In the expression רַךְ הַמֶּזֶג (*rakh ha-mezeg*), temperate, the rabbis used our root to translate into Hebrew the Greek word *istinis*, used for the legal category of "overly sensitive person."

In modern times, Hebrew writer S.Y. Agnon uses the root to describe springtime as מְמֻזָּג (*memuzag*), temperate, i.e., neither hot nor cold. Jewish national poet Hayyim Nahman Bialik metaphorically advises readers that we would be wise לְהִתְמַזֵּג עִם רוּחַ הַדּוֹר (*le-hitmazzeg im ru'ah ha-dor*), "to harmonize with the spirit of one's generation." As a term of art, מֶזֶג (*mezig*), harmony, is found in discussions of symphonic music.

Old-style taverns have a מוֹזֵג (*mozeg*) or מוֹזֶגֶת (*mozeget*), bartender. (In a Hebrew term "borrowed" from English, the feminine of *barman* can also be *barmanit*.) Be careful when using מַזְגָן (*mazgan*) for barkeep: if you request לְהַפְעִיל אֶת הַמַּזְגָן (*le-haph'il et ha-mazgan*), you are simply asking that the air conditioning be turned on. This is because מִזּוּג אֲוִיר (*mizzug avir*), air conditioning, as well as מֶזֶג אֲוִיר (*mezzeg avir*), weather, involves mixing temperatures.

The last word belongs to Bahya Ibn Pakuda (11th century), who observed that the world is held together מִגַּשְׁמִיּוּת וְרוּחָנִיּוּת נִמְזְגוּ (*mi-gashmi'ut ve-ruhani'ut nimzegu*), "by the spiritual and material combined harmoniously." Let's all drink a cup of *mezzeg* to that!

48

It Takes All Kinds

מ-י-נ

mem-yod-nun

W here does manna come from? No, not the miraculous food, which, we are taught, falls from heaven. Rather the question addresses the origin of the Hebrew word מָן (*man*), manna. Exodus suggests an etymology. When the Israelites discover this nutritious seed on the ground they cry out, says the Bible, מָן הוּא (*man hu*). Is this a question, asking מָה הוּא? (*mah hu?*), "What is this?" Or is it, as medieval Hebrew grammarian Yonah Ibn Jannah suggests, an exclamation of surprise at finding a new מִין (*min*), species? For Ibn Jannah, *man* comes from מ-י-נ (*mem, yod, nun*), species. From this root are derived כָּל מִינֵי (*kol minei*), all types of words, including מִיּוּן (*miyyun*), classification; מִינִיּוּת (*miniyyut*), sexuality; and מִינוּת (*minut*), heresy.

In Genesis, the word לְמִינוֹ (*le-mino*), "of every kind"—and others like it—appears ten times in the story of the creation of plants and animals. The root is found in agricultural festivals, such as Sukkot, when we wave the אַרְבָּעָה מִינִים (*arba'ah minim*), four species, and decorate the sukkah with שִׁבְעַת הַמִּינִים (*shivat ha-minim*), seven species of Israel's agricultural products. The root also has kashrut implications. Maimonides, in his laws of forbidden foods, addresses laws linked to מִין בְּמִינוֹ (*min be-mino*), a mixture of permitted and forbidden foods.

To usher out the Sabbath, one uses various מִינֵי בְּשָׂמִים (*minei besamim*), types of spices. A hostess versed in elegant Aramaic will serve מִינֵי תַּרְגִּימָא (*minei targimah*), an assortment of sweetmeats.

It is not difficult to see how the term for "kind" becomes הַמִּין הָאֱנוֹשִׁי (*ha-min ha-enoshi*), the human race, and moves from there to מִין (*min*), gender, dividing the world into masculine and feminine. It is clear that קִיּוּם הַמִּין (*kiyyum ha-min*), survival of the species, requires מְשִׁיכָה מִינִית (*meshikha minit*), sexual attraction, and יַחֲסֵי מִין

(*yahasei min*), sexual concourse. What are to be guarded against are מַחֲלוֹת מִין (*mahalot min*), sexually transmitted diseases. A hospital's emergency room is called חֲדַר מִיּוּן (*hadar miyyun*), because that's where medical emergencies are classified.

How do we get from *min*, species, to *min*, heresy? Scholars suggest that תְּמוּנָה (*temunah*), picture, derives from our root, originally designating a forbidden image—an idol. A מִין (*min*) is a worshiper of these idols. Separating himself from his people, the Jewish heretic, say the rabbis, creates a new מִין (*min*), species of Jew, etymologically similar to but radically different from the new kind of miraculous morsel that was Ibn Jannah's manna.

49

The Text-Message Tradition

מ-ס-ר

mem-samekh-resh

S ometimes it is merely a matter of context. Let's say you are attending a sloppily played basketball game or soccer match in Israel and you hear the Hebrew word מְסִירָה (*mesirah*) bandied about. From the context, you finally realize that they're talking about an errant "pass." Another time, you are walking along a *haredi* neighborhood in Brooklyn and you overhear a conversation about the legality of oral suction during circumcision, laced again with the word *mesirah*. Here, you may assume they're not talking about sports, but about another type of *mesirah*, the religious injunction against handing someone in to the "Roman" authorities.

Both meanings derive from the root מ-ס-ר (*mem, samekh, resh*), to hand over. The root is used in Scripture infrequently, in connection with transgressions and transferring soldiers. It is found most famously in *Pirke Avot*: the rabbinic text asserts that after Moses received the Torah at Sinai, he מְסָרָהּ (*mesarah*), transmitted it, to his disciple Joshua. From this use of the root we derive one of the most important principles of Judaism, handing over the מְסוֹרָה (*mesorah*), tradition, from generation to generation. Note that the word *mesorah* is often used interchangeably with מָסֹרֶת (*masoret*), originally, some say, מַאֲסֹרֶת (*ma'asoret*), bond, from the root א-ס-ר (*alef, samekh, resh*), to bind. Could it be that tradition, where the values of Judaism come from, is as binding as law?

The Conservative branch of Judaism in Israel is called מָסָרְתִּי (*Masorti*), traditional, not to be confused with מְסוֹרָתִי (*mesorati*), applied to traditional, but not movement-affiliated, Israelis. Traditional—and binding—pronunciations of biblical Hebrew come from the בַּעֲלֵי הַמְּסוֹרָה (*ba'alei ha-masorah*), Masoretes (4th–11th century CE). We also find the root in the *Yizkor* service, remembering those who מָסְרוּ אֶת נַפְשָׁם (*masru et nafsham*), gave their lives, for holy causes.

Today's Israeli is quite adept at sending a colleague a cell phone מֶסֶר (*meser*), text message. Be wary of movies containing a מֶסֶר תַּת-סָפִּי (*meser tat-safi*), subliminal message. A drama critic, in yet another context, may write about הַמֶּסֶר שֶׁל הַמַּחֲזֶה (*ha-meser shel ha-mahazeh*), the main point of the play. At a conference, someone can always be seen distributing to participants a תַּמְסִיר (*tamsir*), informational handout. You have certainly come across an individual who, with a great deal of מְסִירוּת (*mesirut*), devotion, מִתְמַסֶּרֶת (*mitmaseret*), dedicates herself, to an organization. Confusingly, a criminal sometimes may מִתְמַסֵּר (*mitmaser*), turn himself in, to the police. And do not confuse *mesirut* with מְסִירוֹת (*mesirot*), a playground game of catch. A good rule of thumb: always think of the context.

50

Finders, Keepers

מ-צ-א

mem-tsadi-alef

The first legal case one studies in Talmud class reads like a rather contemporary allegory. It involves two litigants invoking the principle of "finders, keepers." Each petitioner, claiming ownership, grasps onto the same *talit* and asserts, אֲנִי מְצָאתִיהָ (*ani metsatiha*), "I found it [first]."

Among the more than 400 instances of the root מ-צ-א (*mem, tsadi, alef*), "to find," in Scripture, one finds similarly familiar stories. God, unable לִמְצוֹא (*limtso*), to find, a suitable helpmate for Adam, goes back to the drawing board to create Eve. Noah's dove, after the flood, לֹא מָצְאָה (*lo mats'ah*), was unable to find, a place to rest her feet. When Abraham bargains with God for the souls of Sodom, God assents, saying, אִם אֶמְצָא (*im emtsa*), "should I find [ten righteous people there, I will spare the city]." In a less well-known episode, Joseph, searching for his missing brothers, is himself "found" by a stranger—וַיִּמְצָאֵהוּ אִישׁ (*va-yimtsa'ehu ish*), a mysterious man "comes upon" him, offering help.

Of King Saul it is said jokingly that when as a youth he went looking for his father's asses, וַיִּמְצָאֵהוּ מַלְכוּת (*va-yimtsa'ehu malkhut*), kingship found *him*. The Talmud reports a joke of questionable taste that plays on our root. At weddings, it was customary to ask about the bride: מָצָא אוֹ מוֹצֵא (*matsa o motse?*), Is the bride, as described in Proverbs, "a good *find*?" Or should we apply the misogynistic words of Ecclesiastes, who "*finds* woman bitter"? The Talmud uses the relative clause מַה מָּצִינוּ (*mah matsinu*), "that we have found," when it wants to ascribe similarity to a new situation.

In 1903, Hayyim Nahman Bialik lamented in his poem "On the Slaughter" that after the Kishinev Pogrom he looked for "a path to God," but, he moans, לֹא מְצָאתִיו (*lo metsativ*), "I did not find it."

Today, the root is used in idiomatic expressions, e.g., מוֹצֵא חֵן בְּעֵינַי (*motse hen be-enai*), I like it, literally, it finds favor in my eyes. One who מִתְמַצֵּא (*mitmatse*), is familiar with, his surroundings finds himself comfortable there. The English equivalent of מַמְצִיא (*mamtsi*) is inventor, from *invenire,* Latin for to find. Is it מְצִיאוּתִי (*metsi'uti*), realistic, to look for both הָרָצוּי וְהַמָּצוּי (*ha-ratsu'i ve-ha-matsu'i*), what is desired and what is easily found? Everybody with a little Yiddish likes to find a מְצִיאָה (*metsi'ah*), bargain. If it is not on the shelves, ask about the store's מְצַאי (*metsai*), inventory.

Look for the similar but different root מ-צ-ה (*mem, tsadi, heh*) at Passover time. At the Seder, when you find the *Afikoman,* don't add confusion by yelling, אֲנִי מְצָאתִיהָ (*ani metsatiha*), "I found [the *matzot*]!"

51

Crunching the Numbers

מ-צ-ה

mem-tsadi-heh

L et's take 18 minutes—the halakhic time limit for baking kosher-for-Passover *matsot*—to talk about roots related to the word *matsa*.

Ma'agarim, the online Historical Dictionary of the Hebrew Language Academy (maagarim.hebrew-academy.org.il), firmly insists that the root is מ-צ-צ (*mem, tsadi, tsadi*). Others propose מ-צ-ה (*mem, tsadi, heh*), that root's sister. Both roots mean to press, squeeze or suck out. But would a baker today agree that the dryness of *matsa* is due to the "squeezing" out of its liquid? Lexicographers Mordekhai Rosen and Ernest Klein suggest the root נ-צ-ה (*nun, tsadi, heh*), to hasten. In this case, *matsa* would mean "that which was made in haste," coinciding nicely with the hasty exodus from Egypt, when the bread being baked for the journey didn't have time to rise.

In Scripture, the noun מַצָּה (*matsa*) appears often as a "bread of affliction" and sometimes as a side dish accompanying various sacrificial meals. The verb מָצָה (*matsah*), to squeeze out, is found in a bizarre tale in the book of Judges. Gideon, called by God to deliver Israel from her enemies, challenges Him to soak a fleece fabric with dew while leaving the surrounding grass dry. Next morning, we learn, וַיִּמֶץ טַל (*va-yimmets tal*), "[Gideon] squeezed dew [from the fleece]" and went to war. The root is also found in Leviticus, dealing with the ritual of pigeon sacrifice, where נִמְצָה דָמוֹ (*nimtsa damo*), [the bird's] blood is drained out and then thrown against the altar. Eating *matsa* is a benign ritual in comparison.

The noun מִיץ (*mits*), juice, is so called because it involves squeezing, applying pressure. In Proverbs, we are told, מִיץ חָלָב (*mits halav*), "putting milk under pressure," makes butter. For the wise author, therefore, מִיץ אַפַּיִם (*mits appayim*), putting one's patience under pressure, produces strife. In medical circles, מְצִיצָה (*metsitsa*), taking a drag on a cigarette, has many detractors, as does the מוֹצֵץ (*motsets*), baby pacifier, on which an infant sucks. Today, the act of מְצִיצָה בְּפֶּה (*metsitsa be-peh)*, draining blood orally during ritual circumcision, is the subject of heated religious controversy.

For those who would like to take the lessons of these 18 minutes into the Intermediate Days of the holiday, some recommend to crunch on a piece of chocolate-covered egg *matsa*, מַצָּה עֲשִׁירָה (*matsa ashirah*), literally, enriched *matsa*. Or, take a forkful of מַצִּיָּה (*matsiyyah*), a Hebrew version of Yiddish's *matza brei*. After pouring a cup of boiling water into a תַּמְצִית (*tamtsit*), extract [of tea leaves], and taking a sip, you may contemplate all that *matsa* has wrought.

52

Politics Is Just Like Poetry (Not)

מ-שׁ-ל

mem-shin-lamed

How do we know that politics and poetry don't mix? From Israel's famously engaged writers, who have mastered the art of compartmentalizing: poetry here, politics there. We can also learn this lesson from the root מ-שׁ-ל (*mem, shin, lamed*), which gives us both מָשָׁל (*mashal*), metaphor, and מֶמְשָׁלָה (*memshala*), government.

How two discrete meanings came from the same three letters is shrouded in mystery. One might conjecture the following explanation. An early meaning of the root meant to hold in one's hand and therefore to hold sway over. A metaphor, being a way of getting hold of an abstract idea by comparing it to something tangible, gives one dominion over the idea.

The root comes closest to mixing poetry and politics in the biblical story of Balaam, where the words וַיִּשָּׂא מְשָׁלוֹ וַיֹּאמַר (*va-yissa meshalo va-yomar*), "Taking up his theme, he said," introduces each of Balaam's seven prophecies about affairs of state. In Kings, Solomon is called a מוֹשֵׁל (*moshel*), ruler, and elsewhere is credited with authoring מִשְׁלֵי (*mishlei*), Proverbs. Ezekiel, in a metaphorical diatribe comparing Jerusalem to a harlot, uses our root twice to say כָּל הַמֹּשֵׁל עָלַיִךְ יִמְשֹׁל (*kol ha-moshel alayikh yimshol*), "Everyone who uses metaphors will apply a [non-flattering] proverb to you."

Many rabbinic parables have animals as central figures, as in the genre of מִשְׁלוֹת שׁוּעָלִים (*mishlot shu'alim*), fox fables. The rabbis of the Talmud were careful to characterize the book of Job as a *mashal*, allegory, saying, אִיּוֹב לֹא הָיָה וְלֹא נִבְרָא אֶלָּא מָשָׁל הָיָה (*iyyov lo haya ve-lo nivra, ella mashal haya*), "Job never existed; [the story] was but a parable." In the mystical *Shir ha-Kavod*, chanted during the Shabbat *musaf* service, the congregation declares that although

הַמְשִׁילוּךְ בְּרֹב חֶזְיוֹנוֹת (*himshilukha be-rov hezyonot*), "They compared You in many images," nevertheless You are One.

Two rabbinic sayings using our root have made it into modern Hebrew. When one encounters a metaphor that doesn't quite work, one quotes a Yom Kippur hymn, saying מָשָׁל כְּחֶרֶס הַנִּשְׁבָּר (*mashal ke-heres ha-nishbar*), "It's like a broken piece of pottery." To introduce a comparison, one says, מָשָׁל לְמָה הַדָּבָר דּוֹמֶה? (*mashal le-ma ha-davar domeh*), "You know what this is like?" Like the story of a king, לְמָשָׁל (*le-mashal*), for example, שֶׁאֵין מָשְׁלוֹ (*she-ein moshlo*), who has no peer. When you want to understand the point of a *mashal*, you seek out its נִמְשָׁל (*nimshal*), moral.

We're back to kings and comparisons. Like poetry and politics, however, it's better to keep them apart.

53

You Wash, I'll Dry

נ-ג-ב
nun-gimel-vet

A nyone who has ever mopped a floor in Israel has come into
contact with סְפּוֹנְגְ'ה (*spongia*), to squeegee away the dirty
water. Derived from a Greek word for sponge, the root ס-פ-ג
(*samekh, feh, gimel*), to absorb, has comfortably entered the Hebrew
language. Another root, however, נ-ג-ב (*nun, gimel, vet*), tells an
even more fascinating story, about dryness, arid climes and the
Greek and Yiddish languages.

In Scripture, הַנֶּגֶב (*ha-negev*), the Negev Desert, is a massive
southerly parcel of sun-soaked arid land, cherished by our ancestors.
When Abram and Sarai leave Egypt, after a sexual malentendu with
Pharaoh, they head up, wealthier and wiser, הַנֶּגְבָּה (*ha-negba*),
"toward the Negev." Tinkering with the root's meaning, the story of
Jacob's dream—between a rock and a high ladder—contains the
promise that Jacob's descendants will "spread out," west and east
and north, and also נֶגְבָּה (*negbah*), "to the south."

Today, before eating bread, it is customary to wash one's
hands. The sages of the Talmud (*Sotah 4b*) insist that if one is not
also scrupulous about נִגּוּב יָדַיִם (*nigguv yada'im*), drying the hands, it
is as if one has eaten impure bread.

After a meal, Psalm 126 is chanted on Shabbat and holidays
prior to saying Grace. The Psalm contains a Zionist prayer: that the
Jewish nation shall return speedily to a deserted Land of Israel
כַּאֲפִיקִים בַּנֶּגֶב (*ka-afikim ba-negev*), "like the dried-out rivulets
[wadis] of the Negev," filling swiftly with rainwater after a sudden
cloudburst.

David Ben-Gurion, a fervent promoter of the development
of this area, made his home in the Negev. Among his disciples in
this matter were the pioneering founders of Kibbutz Negba, in 1939,
the southernmost settlement in Mandate Palestine. Negba was the

scene of a furious battle with the Egyptians during the War of Independence, giving rise to the slangy expression חַיּוֹת הַנֶּגֶב (*hayyot ha-negev*), beasts of the Negev, not a reference to the wild animals roaming the area but rather to the fierce demeanor of tough soldiers.

According to Hebrew Language Academy's Ruth Almagor-Ramon, it is to Eliezer Ben-Yehuda that we owe the linguistic triumph, if not the coinage, of the word מַגֶּבֶת (*maggevet*), towel, over *aluntit*, a Greek-derived rabbinic Hebrew synonym. The word מַגְּבִים (*magvim*), windshield wipers, didn't make it into popular Hebrew either, having been shunted aside by a Yiddishism, *visherim*. And then there are the hummus eaters. Nowadays, when you מְנַגֵּב (*menagev*), wipe up, the plate, flourishing a piece of pita, be careful lest some hummus drip to the floor. You don't want to have to do another *spongia*.

54

This Is All Very Touching

נ-ג-ע

nun-gimel-ayin

Psychologists agree that physical touching is an important human activity. The Hebrew language—with the root נ-ג-ע (*nun, gimel, ayin*), to touch—expands the parameters of that activity. A full gamut of meanings is evident in Scripture, beginning with the story of Isaac, who introduces his wife, Rebekah, to King Abimelech as his sister. The king, learning that he has barely escaped committing adultery, announces that anyone הַנֹּגֵעַ (*ha-noge'a*), who touches, Isaac or Rebekah—whether by physical aggression or sexual advances is unclear—will be punished. Touching is further explored in the story of Esther. One may not approach the king unbidden, and it had been a while since the king had called for the queen. But, says Mordecai to Esther, you must save your people; isn't that why הִגַּעַתְּ לַמַּלְכוּת (*higga'at la-malkhut*), "you have ascended to the throne?" Esther ventures forth and the king extends his scepter. Contact is made when וַתִּגַּע בְּרֹאשׁ הַשַּׁרְבִיט (*va-tiga be-rosh ha-sharvit*), "she touched the tip of the scepter."

In Exodus, God uses the root to announce that He will bring עוֹד נֶגַע אֶחָד (*od nega ehad*), "one more plague" upon the Egyptians. Jacob's ladder, in another sense of the root, מַגִּיעַ הַשָּׁמַיְמָה (*magi'a ha-shamayma*), "reaches the Heavens." In Leviticus, we learn that אִם לֹא תַגִּיעַ יָדוֹ (*im lo taggi'a yado*), literally "if his hands do not reach that far," meaning if one hasn't the means to sacrifice a sheep, he may bring something of lesser value. Ethics of the Fathers teaches not to judge another עַד שֶׁתַּגִּיעַ לִמְקוֹמוֹ (*ad she-taggi'a li-mekomo*), "until you have reached his place." The *Sheheheyanu* blessing praises God that הִגִּעָנוּ לַזְּמַן הַזֶּה (*higgi'anu la-zeman ha-zeh*), He has brought us to this time.

Today, a business letter might begin with בְּנוֹגֵעַ לְבַקָּשָׁתְךָ (*be-noge'a le-bakashatekha*), regarding your request. At the water cooler, you might hear about a coworker's promotion and think, מַגִּיעַ לָהּ (*magiya la*), she deserves it, literally, it's coming to her. But if you are נוֹגֵעַ בַּדָּבָר (*noge'a ba-davar*), directly involved in the matter, you might choose to excuse yourself from the discussion.

Some people prefer עֲדָשׁוֹת מַגָּע (*adeshot magga*), contact lenses, to glasses. These days, one might want to learn קְרַב מַגָּע (*kerav magga*), an Israeli system of self-defense. At the museum, you may see a sign warning אַל גַּעַת (*al ga'at*), do not touch. And then there is a שׁוֹמֵר נְגִיעָה (*shomer negi'a*), one who observes a restriction against premarital touching. Obviously, some people can be touched spiritually without touching physically.

55

Shake It? Just Take It

נ-ט-ל

nun-tet-lamed

A t a campsite in the Galilee during Sukkot, a young man "borrows" a palm branch and citron—*lulav* and *etrog*—lying on a table. He picks them up, holds them to his chest and, neither making a blessing nor waving the *lulav*, returns them to the table. Did he fulfill the holiday's mitzva of נְטִילַת לוּלָב (*netilat lulav*), "taking the lulav"? Etymologically, at least, he did, since נְטִילָה (*netilah*) has to do with taking, not shaking. What about נְטִילַת יָדַיִם (*netilat yadayim*), handwashing? What is taken here? Is it perhaps the נַטְלָה (*natlah*), laver, from which one pours purifying water on the hands? Or maybe it is the hands that are indeed taken—from the profane to the sacred realm?

Scripture scarcely uses the root נ-ט-ל (*nun, tet, lamed*), to take, carry off. For Isaiah, the verb וַיְנַטְלֵם (*va-yenatlem*), reminds us that God has removed us from distress. The prophet Zephaniah uses נְטִילֵי כָסֶף (*netilei kessef*), for the rich, i.e., those "laden" with silver. And Proverbs suggests נֵטֶל הַחוֹל (*netel ha-hol*), the heaviness of sand, as a metaphor for problems caused by fools.

Hebrew lexicographer Eliezer Ben-Yehuda cites hundreds of instances where our root is found in rabbinic literature, from the prosaic נוֹטֵל צִפָּרְנַיִם (*notel tsipornayim*), fingernail clipper, to the talmudic meditation on the soul, acknowledging that אַתָּה עָתִיד לִטְּלָה מִמֶּנִּי (*atah atid litla mimmeni*), "You will eventually take [my soul] from me." Moving from the spiritual to the material, the Talmud asks, what's worthier, giving charity to an entrepreneur or investing in the business? One rabbi responded with our root to suggest that a נוֹטֵל בַּכִּיס (*notel ba-kis*), "a patron in one's own pocket," i.e., an investor, is more praiseworthy than a lender or contributor. When talmudic rabbis took offense at holier-than-thou criticism of their religious behavior, they used our root to formulate a rejoinder. In response to a gently euphemistic "Take the toothpick from between your teeth," they answered, caustically, טֹל קוֹרָה מִבֵּין עֵינֶיךָ (*tol korah mi-bein einekha*), "Remove the heavy piece of lumber from between your eyes," i.e., Worry about your own (bigger) faults.

Using a variation of the root, the government מַטִּילָה מִסִּים (*mattilah missim*), levies taxes, while a hen מַטִּילָה בֵּיצִים (*mattilah beitsim*), lays eggs. At a cafe in Israel, sidle up to the barista and, omitting direct reference to coffee, caffeine or milk fat, just order הָפוּךְ נָטוּל וְדַל (*hafukh natul ve-dal*), literally, "upside down," "taken away" and "unrich." You'll be served a low-fat decaffeinated cappuccino. Take it and sip it.

56

A Little Traveling Music, Please

נ-ס-ע

nun-samekh-ayin

How do we know it's a mitzva to travel? At the Red Sea, God commands Moses to instruct the reluctant Children of Israel to get a move on, saying, וְיִסָּעוּ (*ve-yissa'u*), "Let them go forward." Although the root נ-ס-ע (*nun, samekh, ayin*) means to travel, there is convincing evidence that it was used originally to describe the quarrying of rocks. So how did we "travel" from there to here? Quarrying involves pulling up stones. Similarly, one pulls up tent pegs to strike camp and set out on a journey.

For 40 years the Israelites encamped and struck camp alternatively while traveling from Egypt to the banks of the Jordan. Scripture uses the expression וַיִּסְעוּ...וַיַּחֲנוּ (*va-yisu...va-yahanu*), "they traveled...they encamped," over and over again in *Parashat* מַסְעֵי (*masei*), describing their travels. The most famous verse using our root is one we chant in synagogue today when we take out the Torah, וַיְהִי בִּנְסֹעַ הָאָרֹן (*va-yehi binso'a ha-aron*), "When the Ark set forward."

Today, the root is found in the nouns נוֹסֵעַ (*nose'a*), traveler, and נְסִיעָה (*nesiya*), voyage. The latter word is part of the hearty wish נְסִיעָה טוֹבָה (*nesiya tova*), bon voyage. Israeli scouts participate in an annual מַסָּע מִיָּם אֶל יָם (*massa mi-yam el yam*), march from sea to sea. Chess pieces move only short distances, but a move in the game is also a מַסָּע (*massa*). Let us not forget the מַסָּעוֹת (*massa'ot*), travels, of the Jews' most famous traveler, Benjamin of Tudela. And he didn't even have access to a סוֹכֵן נְסִיעוֹת (*sokhen nesiyot*), travel agent.

An Israeli will frequently ask a friend for a הַסָּעָה (*hassa'a*), ride. Although the word נֶסַע (*nesa*) is also on the books for a ride in the sense of a "lift," the word you'll hear most frequently for that activity is טְרֶמְפּ (*tremp*), hitchhike. Are there pills, nowadays, for קַדַּחַת נְסִיעָה (*kaddahat nesiya*), slang for pre-travel jitters?

An impatient Israeli will jump into the passenger seat and yell סַע! (*sa*), "Go!" On the other hand, laconic Israeli vocalist Arik Einstein sings a slow-paced ballad called סַע לְאַט (*sa le'at*), "Drive Slowly." Playing on that expression, Pizza Hut, when it opened in Israel, distributed bumper stickers with the suggestion סַע לַהָאט (*sa la-hat*), "Drive to the Hut." Nowadays, with the development of the Israeli railroad system, one can find parking lots with signs reading חֲנֵה וְסַע (*haneh ve-sa*), Park 'n' Ride.

Modes of locomotion and destinations may change but, from ancient Israelites to modern Israelis, Hebraically we haven't traveled all that far.

57

That's a Lock

נ-ע-ל
nun-ayin-lamed

Y om Kippur provides an opportunity for taking stock of one's soul. It is also a good time to examine the ways of the Hebrew language. Take the example of נְעִילָה (*ne'ila*), a word used for the Yom Kippur prohibition against wearing leather shoes, נְעִילַת הַסַּנְדָּל (*neilat ha-sandal*), and, at the same time, the name of the concluding service of the Day of Atonement.

How did this surprising juxtaposition come about? In the beginning, the root נ-ע-ל (*nun, ayin, lamed*) was used to denote an act of closing. This sense can be understood in a metaphor in the Song of Songs: my beloved is a גַּן נָעוּל (*gan na'ul*), enclosed garden. In Scripture as well as in modern speech a מַנְעוּל (*man'ul*) is a lock, as in S.Y. Agnon's love story collection, עַל כַּפּוֹת הַמַּנְעוּל (*al kapot ha-man'ul*), *At the Handles of the Lock*, a title borrowed from the Song of Songs.

In rabbinic literature, the Talmud says that a דֶּלֶת נִנְעֶלֶת (*delet nin'elet*), locked door, does not open quickly, and a midrash teaches that all the words of the Torah need one another because מַה שֶּׁזֶּה נוֹעֵל (*ma she-zeh no'el*), what one locks or hides, another opens or reveals.

In the world of computers, the word *ne'ila*, locking, is used to describe the addition of a code to a file that prevents it from being changed or erased.

So how does locking lead to putting on shoes? According to one grammarian, putting on shoes is an act of enclosure. And so we come to a rich storehouse of words using our root for הַנְעָלָה (*han'ala*), footwear: נַעֲלֵי בַּיִת (*na'alei bayit*) are slippers; נַעֲלֵי ספּוֹרט (*na'alei sport*), sneakers; נַעֲלֵי אֵילַת (*na'alei eilat*), flip-flops; נַעֲלֵי גּוֹלְדָּה (*na'alei golda*) are oxfords like those worn by Golda Meir; and

נַעֲלֵי יָד (*na'alei yad*) is an old expression for gloves, now fallen into disuse.

When, in Genesis, the King of Sodom offers Abraham spoils of war, the proud forefather-to-be refuses even a שְׂרוֹךְ נַעַל (*serokh na'al*), sandal strap. Moses' first encounter with God, at the Burning Bush, is in the form of a voice saying שַׁל נְעָלֶיךָ (*shal ne'alekha*), remove your sandals. And then there is חֲלִיצַת הַנַּעַל (*halitsat ha-na'al*), an ancient ceremony that symbolically frees a man from the biblical obligation to marry his brother's childless widow—where she removes his shoe.

We rarely walk in those נַעֲלַיִם (*na'alayim*), shoes, anymore, but there is always someone who will נוֹעֵל אֶת הַיְשִׁיבָה (*no'el et ha-yeshiva*), bring the meeting to a close. And the column as well.

58

Help Is on the Way

נ-צ-ל

nun-tsadi-lamed

A high school teacher—a Hebrew language purist—takes his class for an outing to a nearby lake. A mediocre swimmer, he gets caught in an undertow, but when he shouts הוֹשִׁיעוּ (*hoshi'u*), help!, the students pay no attention. Why? Because they recognize the SOS call only in modern Hebrew: הַצִּילוּ (*hatsilu*), save me!

The root נ-צ-ל (*nun, tsadi, lamed*), from which *hatsilu* derives, originally meant "to pluck out from" and then eventually "to save" and "to make use of."

Several modern expressions using this root come from classical texts. Visiting the cemetery, you might hear a beggar quote a line from Proverbs, צְדָקָה תַּצִּיל מִמָּוֶת (*tsedaka tatsil mi-mavet*), "Righteousness [i.e., charity] preserves from death." The word הַצָּלָה (*hatsala*), deliverance, used today as the name of a Jewish emergency medical service, can be found in Mordecai's admonition of Esther, alerting her that if she does not come to the aid of her people, *hatsala* will surely come from another source. A נִצּוֹל הַשּׁוֹאָה (*nitsol ha-sho'a*), Holocaust survivor, is often described metaphorically in Shoah literature with a phrase taken from Zechariah: אוּד מֻצָּל מֵאֵשׁ (*ud mutsal me-esh*), "a brand plucked from the fire."

The Hebrew teacher in our story would have been well advised to invite a מַצִּיל (*matsil*), lifeguard, to his outing. But he probably knew the word *matsil* mainly from the story told by the Wise Woman of Tekoa in II Samuel—to arouse David's compassion for his own son—of her two sons fighting, one of whom gets killed because אֵין מַצִּיל בֵּינֵיהֶם (*ein matsil beineihem*), "there is none to pull them apart."

In Midian, Jethro's daughters report, Moses הִצִּילָנוּ (*hitsilanu*), "saved us," from marauding shepherds. When today one hears a story of a particularly dangerous situation, one cries out, in Aramaic, רַחֲמָנָא לִצְּלַן (*rahamana litslan*), may the Merciful One save us, from such circumstances. Another sense of the root is not quite so delicate. One who uses other people is called a נַצְלָן (*natslan*), exploiter. This sense is found in Exodus, where we are told of the Israelites, וַיְנַצְּלוּ אֶת מִצְרָיִם (*va-yenatselu et mitsrayim*), "they despoiled the Egyptians." Businesspeople might take advantage of a price differential, as in נִיצוּל פְּעָרִים (*nitsul pe'arim*), arbitrage.

There are certainly more ways that modern Hebrew makes use of our root. If important expressions have been omitted here, there is always the reflexive form of the verb לְהִתְנַצֵּל (*le-hitnatsel*), to apologize. With this derivation one can even be extricated from blame.

59

A Hole in (More Than) One

נ-ק-ב

nun-kof-vet

What do flutes, pores, pierced ears, mallets, curses and train conductors have in common? They are all related to the root ב—ק—נ (*nun, khof, vet*), to perforate. In Hebrew, a נֶקֶב (*nekev*), hole, covers a wide spectrum. There is the talmudic נֶקֶב הַמַּחַט (*nekev ha-mahat*), eye of the needle, through which one pushes an elephant—symbolizing convoluted reasoning.

To make music with a recorder, one's fingers play on the instrument's נְקָבִים (*nekavim*), holes. Other *nekavim*, perforations, on the lungs of a slaughtered animal, render it unkosher. There are holes on human skin, נַקְבּוּבִים (*nakbuvim*), pores, through which one excretes impurities. In the *Asher Yatsar* blessing, recited on emerging from the lavatory, one praises God for having created human beings with נְקָבִים נְקָבִים (*nekavim nekavim*), many apertures, necessary for bodily functions.

Other types of holes can be traced to our root, like a נִקְבָּה (*nikbah*), tunnel. On the train, the conductor uses his מַקֵּב (*makkav*), hole-puncher, to acknowledge your ticket. For some, נִקּוּב אָזְנַיִם (*nikkuv oznayim*), ear piercing, is a rite of passage. Remember the holes of IBM punch cards at college registration? In Hebrew, the procedure was called נַקְבָנוּת (*nakvanut*), key punching. A carpenter's tool that gouges wood is a מַקֶּבֶת (*makkevet*), mallet. Some say this word explains why Judah, the hero of Maccabean fame, is called הַמַּקַּבִּי (*ha-makkabi*), the Hammer.

The root appears in a biblical allusion to the creation of the two genders, זָכָר וּנְקֵבָה (*zakhar u-nekevah*), masculine and feminine. A midrash declares that this refers to one body, created with corresponding male and female parts.

The verb נָקַב (*nakav*) often indicates outrageous speech. The Talmud characterizes Moses, normally sympathetic, as callous in rendering justice, attributing to him the enigmatic expression יִקֹּב הַדִּין אֶת הָהָר (*yikkov ha-din et ha-har*), "Let justice make a gash in the mountain." The verb also designates another form of outrageous speech, blasphemy. Leviticus prescribes the death penalty for one who נֹקֵב שֵׁם ה' (*nokkev shem ha-shem*), curses God's name.

In Numbers, to justify his refusal of Balak's summons to curse the Israelites, Balaam asks, מָה אֶקֹּב לֹא קַבֹּו אֵ-ל (*mah ekkov lo kabo e-l*), "Why should I curse whom God has not cursed?" The verb is also used in naming. After 14 years of service, Jacob asks for wages from his father-in-law, whom לֹא נָקֹב בְּשֵׁם (*lo nikov be-shem*), we shall not name. Deviously, the scoundrel proposes נָקְבָה שְׂכָרְךָ (*nakvah sekharkha*), "Name your price." That a canny Jacob defeats this shady dealmaker remains a cause for optimism today.

60

How to Attack a Problem

נ-ק-פ

nun-kof-feh

picturesque fall scene in Israel: two Arab women in Jerusalem's Independence Park, dressed in black from head to toe, aggressively beating olive trees with sticks. In classical Hebrew, this activity, נֹקֵף (*nokef*), beating fruit from a tree, is picturesque in another way as well. First of all, the root נ-ק-פ (*nun, kof, feh*), to beat, is identical to another root—except for its meaning. Secondly, the similar root, ת-ק-פ (*tav, kof, feh*), to assault or overpower, has derivations that parallel those of *nun, kof, feh*.

It is in Isaiah that we first encounter the agrarian setting of the root, in the expression כְּנֹקֶף זַיִת (*ke-nokef zayit*), "like the shaking of the olive tree" for gleaning. Today, to describe a detached observer, one might remark לֹא נָקַף בְּאֶצְבַּע (*lo nakaf be-etsba*), he didn't lift a finger. Subsequently, however, נָקְפוּ לִבּוֹ (*nekafo libbo*), he felt remorse.

In the book of Esther, the related root *tav, kof, peh* describes מַעֲשֵׂה תָקְפּוֹ (*ma'aseh tokpo*), the powerful acts, of Ahasuerus. Queen Esther herself writes a letter for the purpose of confirming, אֶת כָּל תֹּקֶף (*et kol tokef*), with full authority, a previous letter written by Mordecai.

The root is also found in one of the most beautiful hymns of the High Holiday service, וּנְתַנֶּה תֹּקֶף (*u-netaneh tokef*), "Let us communicate the power" of the day's holiness. It also has a place toward the end of the Passover haggadah, in the expression תַּקִּיף הוּא (*takkif hu*), "Mighty is He," found in a song in praise of God's power.

In everyday speech, a brutish person is תּוֹקְפָנִי (*tokfani*), pugnaciously aggressive, and a הַתְקָפָה (*hatkafa*), assault, may cause a person in fragile health to suffer a הַתְקָפַת לֵב (*hatkafat lev*), heart attack. In formal speech, הַשּׁוֹדֵד תָּקַף (*ha-shoded takaf*), the highwayman attacked, but also הַנּוֹעֵם תָּקַף (*ha-no'em takaf*), the speaker condemned.

As to the yeshiva boy in the study hall, גַּעְגּוּעִים תָּקְפוּ עָלָיו (*ga'gu'im takfu alav*), longings (for home) overwhelmed him; הַשֵּׁנָה תְּקָפָה אוֹתוֹ (*ha-shena takfa oto*), sleep overtook him; and תָּקְפָה עָלָיו מִשְׁנָתוֹ (*takfa alav mishnato*), his studies became too hard for him.

Today, a person may be תַּקִּיף (*takkif*), firm and resolute, and a passport is either תָּקֵף (*takef*), valid, or לֹא בַּר תֹּקֶף (*lo bar tokef*), invalid. When security measures were more lax, one might arrive in Israel only to have the inspector look at his passport and announce פָּג תָּקְפּוֹ (*pag tokpo*), it has expired. One knew then he might not be seeing any picturesque scenes in Israel on that trip.

61

I Get, Therefore I Give

נ-ת-נ

nun-tav-nun

When the New World Pilgrims celebrated their first harvest, they borrowed from Judaism both the festival of Sukkot and Judaism's emphasis on giving thanks. Just think of the English word Thanksgiving and the Hebrew expression לָתֵת הוֹדָיָה (*la-tet hodayya*), to give thanks. Quirkily, לָתֵת has lost both the first and last letters of its three-letter root, נ-ת-נ (*nun, tav, nun*), to give.

We know of humankind's terrestrial responsibilities from the psalm that tells us הָאָרֶץ נָתַן לִבְנֵי אָדָם (*ha-aretz natan livnei adam*), "The earth He gave to mankind." Ethical behavior is implied metaphorically in the verse לִפְנֵי עִוֵּר לֹא תִתֵּן מִכְשֹׁל (*lifnei ivver lo titten mikhshol*), "Do not put a stumbling block before the blind." Like Job, we resign ourselves to fate when, learning of a death, we say, ה' נָתַן וְה' לָקָח (*Hashem natan ve-Hashem lakah*), "God has given and God has taken away."

That the first Jewish professor of architecture was Bezalel, the builder of the tabernacle, we discover from וּלְהוֹרֹת נָתַן בְּלִבּוֹ (*u-le-horot natan be-libbo*), "[God] instilled in his heart to teach." The Israelites in the desert constantly complained to Moses, using our root to grumble נִתְּנָה רֹאשׁ (*nitna rosh*), either "Let's head back" or "Let us give ourselves a new leader." Moses reacts both humbly and wearily to this carping; when Joshua complains that people are usurping Moses' prophecy powers, Moses replies, מִי יִתֵּן (*mi yitten*), "Would it were" that all Israelites were prophets as well.

The root is linked to several Jewish holidays. One of the mitzvot of Purim is מַתָּנוֹת לָאֶבְיֹנִים (*mattanot la-evyonim*), gifts to the poor. On Simhat Torah we sing תְּנוּ כָּבוֹד לַתּוֹרָה (*tenu kavod la-tora*), give honor to the Torah. Shavuot is celebrated as זְמַן מַתַּן תּוֹרָתֵנוּ (*zeman mattan torateinu*), the Season of the Giving of our Law.

If some men consider themselves God's gift to the Jewish people, who can blame them? Just look at the surfeit of names proclaiming just that. Among others, there are מַתִּתְיָהוּ (*mattityahu*), Matthew; יְהוֹנָתָן (*yehonatan*), Jonathan; and נְתַנְאֵל (*netanel*), Nathaniel—all "gifts of God."

In Israel, the root helps us to realize the importance of מַשָּׂא וּמַתָּן (*massa u-mattan*), negotiation, even between the country's נְתִינִים (*netinim*), citizens. Not every project is נִתָּן לְבִצּוּעַ (*nittan le-vitsu'a*), feasible, and not every problem can be resolved using נְתוּנִים (*netunim*), data, literally "givens." Sometimes it's necessary לָתֵת צָ'נְס (*la-tet tshans*), to take a chance and permit a do-over. That's how we got Thanksgiving, after all, by doing over the holiday of Sukkot.

62

Round and Round We Go

ס-ב-ב

samekh-vet-vet

If you've ever witnessed the Sufi dance of the whirling dervishes, you understand how twirling in circles can lead to religious ecstasy. Perhaps that is one reason that Moses, at the giving of the Ten Commandments, was told וְהִגְבַּלְתָּ אֶת הָעָם סָבִיב (*ve-higbalta et haam saviv*), "Have the people circle [Sinai] round about." Perhaps that is also why the Hebrew root ס-ב-ב (*samekh, vet, vet*), which has three main related meanings—to surround, to turn around and to attend a banquet—holds such a central place in the Jewish tradition.

The psalmist echoes the call to Moses by chanting סֹבּוּ צִיּוֹן וְהַקִּיפוּהָ (*sobu tsiyyon ve-hakifuha*), encircle Mount Zion round about. A second use is found in the Hallel service, where we sing that at the time of the Exodus the Jordan River יִסֹּב לְאָחוֹר (*yisov le-ahor*), turned around and flowed backward.

And the third meaning? That's an interesting linguistic story. At the Passover Seder, the youngest child uses our root to ask why we are seated כֻּלָּנוּ מְסֻבִּין (*kulanu mesubin*), all of us leaning to the left side. How did encircling get to mean leaning? It appears that in days of old, one would sit down to a מְסָבָּה (*mesiba*), banquet, at a round table (think of King Arthur). Aristocrats would sit down to a festive meal on dining couches set around a circle of small tables. Because sitting on cushions is conducive to lounging, the word מְסֻבִּין (*mesubin*), seated at a banquet, came to also mean reclining.

In modern times, you can tell that a municipality is enlightened if it shows concern for אֵיכוּת הַסְּבִיבָה (*eikhut ha-seviva*), the quality of its physical surroundings. Today, you don't need a סִבָּה (*sibba*), reason (turn of affairs), to have a מְסָבָּה (*mesiba*), party. Some people get dizzy when they use the word מְסָבָּה (*mesiba*) to mean spiral staircase.

To induce further vertigo, the Hebrew Language Academy tells us to distinguish between לַעֲשׂוֹת סִבּוּב (*la'asot sivuv*), to go for a stroll, and לַעֲשׂוֹת סִבּוּב (*la'asot sibuv*), to turn a screw. Hebrew causes our heads to spin even more when we realize that לְהִסְתּוֹבֵב (*le-histovev*) means both to go about from place to place and to turn around. Speaking of spinning, let us not forget the Hanukkah סְבִיבוֹן (*sevivon*), *dreidel*.

And then there are those Israeli folk dances set to songs with refrains that contain our root, like נְסוֹבֵב אֶת הָהָר (*ne-sovev et ha-har*), "Let's go round the mountain," and סוֹבִּי, סוֹבִּי, מַמְטֵרָה (*sobi, sobi, mamtera*), "Twirl, twirl, water sprinkler." Ecstasy, it appears, also comes when you celebrate in song and dance the reclamation of the land.

63

Signs of the Times

ס-מ-נ

samekh-mem-nun

Hapax Legomena, words that appear only once in the Bible, are troublesome, giving few hints as to their meaning. Take the example of the word נִסְמָן (*nisman*), found only in an agricultural parable in Isaiah. What can the prophet mean when he asserts that barley, unlike other grains, is *nisman*? Perhaps the fact that the root ס-מ-נ (*samekh, mem, nun*), sign or mark, is used in many subsequent derivations will throw some light on the matter.

In rabbinic literature, the word סִימָנִים (*simanim*) can mean signs of a chicken's ritual cleanness, a mnemonic device, character traits that identify the Jewish people, or the numbered paragraphs of the Code of Jewish Law. The Talmud suggests an alternative name for Mount Sinai, a הַר סִימָנַאי (*har simanai*), Mount of Signs, asking to be deciphered. Ever notice the two inverted letters *nun*, before and after Numbers 10:35-36? Rashi calls them סִימָנִיּוֹת (*simaniyyot*), signs to Rashi that these verses are "misplaced."

There are dozens of expressions that include the word סִימָן (*siman*), mark, for example: סִימָן קְרִיאָה (*siman keri'ah*), exclamation point; סִימָן שְׁאֵלָה (*siman she'elah*), question mark; and סִימָנֵי פִּיסוּק (*simanei pisuk*), punctuation marks. In today's computer-centered world, where there is more than one way to use a סִימָנִיָּה (*simaniyyah*), bookmark, who can imagine living without the סַמָּן (*samman*), cursor? Some GPS directions often include a סִמְנוֹף (*simannof*), landmark, or two. The only use, however, for an אֲסִימוֹן (*asimon*), Israeli public telephone token, in today's smartphone society is as a pendant for a necklace.

Not all is high tech, however. If you still receive a paper paycheck, you can hold it up to the light to see a סִימָן מַיִם (*siman mayyim*), watermark. Away from the computer, a teenager will show biological סִימָנֵי בַּגְרוּת (*simanei bagrut*), signs of puberty. A patient will still present a תִּסְמֹנֶת (*tismonet*), symptom, even without a CT scan. You don't need a weather map to know that when the sky is overcast, מִסְתַּמֵּן (*mistamen*), it's a sign, that rain is coming.

Traditional sayings are constantly being updated, as מַעֲשֵׂה אֲבוֹת סִימָן לְבָנִים (*ma'aseh avot siman le-vanim*), "the deeds of our ancestors prefigure those of subsequent generations," becomes "Like father, like son." The rabbinic cliché that בַּת תְּחִלָּה סִימָן יָפֶה לְבָנִים (*bat tehillah siman yafeh le-vanim*), "a first-born daughter is a nice sign that sons will follow," is taken as "an older sister is good for boys." The traditional בְּסִימָן טוֹב וּבְמַזָּל טוֹב (*be-siman tov u-ve-mazzal tov*), "under a good sign [of the Zodiac]," suggests "Lots of luck!" After all, some people, like some words—and some of Isaiah's *nisman* barley—are just lucky.

64

Soaking It Up

ס-פ-ג

samekh-feh-gimel

Have you heard about the latest Hanukkah miracle? Some bakeries in Israel are claiming that סוּפְגָּנִיּוֹת (*sufganiyyot*), jelly donuts, are healthful.

We won't go into the validity of this claim about the traditional pastry used to celebrate the miracle of Hanukkah in the Jewish state. We are concerned here only with the way the root ס-פ-ג (*samekh, feh, gimel*), to absorb, sits at the center of this delicacy.

This root, which comes from the Greek for sponge, is not found in the Bible. It is, however, sprinkled all over rabbinic literature, where we learn that before the jelly donut there was a סוּפְגָּנִית (*sufganit*), a prototype of today's sponge cake. The rabbis of *Pirke Avot* used the root metaphorically, indicating that among the four types of students is the סְפוֹג (*sefog*), sponge, the type who סוֹפֵג אֶת הַכֹּל (*sofeg et ha-kol*), absorbs everything that is taught, including the trivial and the false. Aside from its presence in rabbinic thought, the root was found in daily life, e.g., at the bathhouse, where it was the job of the סַפָּג (*sappag*), bath attendant, to towel off the bather. Rabbi Hanina loosened a halakic knot by declaring that, indeed, מִסְתַּפְגִין (*mistapgin*), one may dry oneself with a towel on Shabbat. Much rabbinic ink is spilled in another halakhic debate, about the number of lashes a sinner סוֹפֵג (*sofeg*), absorbs, in punishment.

In her song "*Hevelei Mashiah*" ("Birth Pangs of the Messiah"), Naomi Shemer exhibits charming sweetness when using our verb to describe Jewish tribulations. When she writes, אֲנִי סוֹפֵג מַכָּה אַחַר מַכָּה (*ani sofeg makkah ahar makkah*), "I endure blow after blow," this national adversity signals the coming of the Messiah. In his monumental 1958 novel, *Days of Ziklag*, about the birth pangs of the State of Israel during the War of Independence, S. Yizhar adapts the root to modern times when a soldier tells his battle-weary comrades הִסְפִּיגוּ לָכֶם כַּהֹגֶן (*hispigu lakhem ka-hogen*), "They gave it to you but good!"

Today, one may use the word מַסְפֵּג (*maspeg*) for blotter. Only a purist who delights in etymology would use *maspeg* for tampon or סְפִיגָה (*sefigah*) for osmosis. Back in the day, פִּטְרִיּוֹת (*pitriyyot*), mushrooms—because they are very absorbent—were called סְפוֹגִים (*sefogim*). The purist who lived in a humid climate could use a סוֹפֵג לַחוּת (*sofeg lahut*), dehumidifier, or, when driving on a bumpy road, סַפָּג זַעֲזוּעִים (*sappag za'azu'im*), shock absorbers.

A piece of challa is all that is necessary for the person who contentedly סוֹפֵג (*sofeg*), sops up, the gravy on his plate. And so, after all this, we are back to "healthful" eating.

65

Safek News

A re all the Hebrew words that are derived from the same three-letter root necessarily related to each other? While many linguists go to great lengths to harmonize conflicts, there is room for doubt. Take the example of the root ס-פ-ק (*samekh, feh, kof*), which is applied, variously, to expressions of doubt, considerations of supply and demand, clapping one's hands (in anger or in joy) and the act of tying two ends of a rope.

A look at the sources is instructive. After 40 years of wandering in the desert, the Israelites prepare to enter Canaan by crossing through the kingdom of Moab. Fearful of being conquered by a formidable Israelite army, the Moabite king Balak summons Balaam, a prophet known for the efficacy of his curses, to put a curse on the Israelites. Instead, Balaam blesses them. The story's narrator uses our root (borrowed from an Arabic word for slapping someone in the face) to focus on Balak's reaction to this turn of events וַיִּסְפֹּק אֶת כַּפָּיו (*va-yispok et kappav*), the king clapped his hands in anger. The root takes on a different nuance in a later rabbinic prohibition, often ignored today: לֹא מְסַפְּקִין (*lo me-sapkin*), one may not clap on Shabbat, even on joyous occasions. It is possible, but doubtful, that "putting the hands together" in applause is similar to tying two ends of a rope together, as in בִּמְסַפֵּק חֶבֶל עַל חֶבֶל (*be-messapek hevel al hevel*), when one ties one end of a rope to another.

Still another use of the root, relating to sufficiency, provides an ample supply of derivations, from סַפָּק (*sappak*), purveyor of goods, to אַסְפָּקָה (*aspaka*), supply. *Pirke Avot* (1:16) hints—with an enigmatic use of our root—that every rabbi should have a personal rabbi וְהִסְתַּלֵּק מִן הַסָּפֵק (*ve-histalek min ha-safek*), "and remove yourself from doubt." Hebrew University professor Avigdor Shinan explains that this means that a rabbi uncertain of his own halakhic decision should have a rabbi "of his own" for consultation.

According to etymologist Ernest Klein, the word סָפֵק (*safek*), doubt itself, is—in an ironic twist—"of uncertain origin." Thus one should be מְסֻפָּק (*mesupak*), dubious; and a סַפְקָן (*safkan*), skeptic; and have סְפֵקוּת (*sefekut*), hesitation about what is סַפְקָנִי (*safkani*), unlikely. And the author illustrates the difficulty in harmonizing the different derivations of our root by proposing the following tongue twister: סָפֵק אִם הַסַּפָּק הִסְפִּיק לִסְפּוֹק אֶת כַּפָּיו (*safek im ha-sappak hispik li-spok et kappav*), "It is not clear if the supplier had occasion to clap his hands."

Are you מִסְתַּפֵּק בְּמֻעָט (*mistappek be-mu'at*), satisfied with little? If so, just shout out this word to those who want to give you more: מַסְפִּיק (*maspik*), Enough!

66

Sharing Secrets

ס-ת-ר

samekh-tav-resh

There are two types of people in this world: those who believe only in what they see and those who look for truths hidden behind the merely visible. The Hebrew root ס-ת-ר (*samekh, tav, resh*), to hide or conceal, covers hidden things with a wide blanket. In Scripture, the root is found in several contexts. Using the most literal and obvious meaning of the root, I Samuel tells us that David מִסְתַּתֵּר (*mistater*), "is hiding," from King Saul's murderous intentions. In Psalms, David uses the root metaphorically, praying that God יַסְתִּירֵנִי בְּסֵתֶר כְּנָפָיו (*yastireini be-seter kenafav*), "will shelter me in the protection of His wings." When Deuteronomy proclaims that הַנִּסְתָּרוֹת (*ha-nistarot*), "the hidden things," belong to God, the Torah is asserting its opposition to esoteric speculation.

At the Burning Bush, וַיַּסְתֵּר מֹשֶׁה פָּנָיו (*va-yaster moshe panav*), "Moses hid his face," because he was afraid to gaze at God's countenance. The expression הֶסְתֵּר פָּנִים (*hester panim*), hiding the Divine face, is used to communicate the withdrawal of God's protection from His people and is brought into play by theologians to explain catastrophes that have befallen the Jews. Post-biblical commentators link the name אֶסְתֵּר (*ester*), Esther, which they trace to our root, to the non-appearance of God's name in the narrative of her book.

One form of our root is found in the Siddur, which calls on mankind to behave properly both בְּסֵתֶר וּבְגָלוּי (*be-seter u-ve-galui*), in private and public settings. While the word סְתִירָה (*setira*), contradiction, is likely to come from another root entirely, the Talmud's discussion of the *sota*, adulterous wife, takes the word *setira* from our root to refer to a sexual assignation, an action most often performed in secret. A private investigator in this case might want to write his top-secret report in דְּיוֹ סְתָרִים (*deyo setarim*), invisible ink.

One of the highest forms of benevolence in Judaism is מַתָּן בְּסֵתֶר (*matan be-seter*), discreetly given charity, where the donor elects to remain unidentified. Anonymity is also a value in the Jewish folk belief that the undistinguished-looking person sitting next to you on the bus may turn out to be a נִסְתָּר (*nistar*), a hidden saint.

One of the mysteries of the Hebrew language is the word מִסְתּוֹר (*mistor*), mystery. Is the English word "mystery" related to our root? It is likely that we will need חָכְמַת הַנִּסְתָּר (*hokhmat ha-nistar*), the ancient wisdom of the unseen, otherwise known as קַבָּלָה (*kabbala*), Kabbalah, to reply to that question. Let's talk about Kabbalah and its root in another chapter. Until then, we'll keep it a secret.

67

Crossing Over

ע-ב-ר

ayin-vet-resh

Why did the Hebrew cross the road? Because that is literally what an עִבְרִי (*ivri*), Hebrew, does. An original *ivri*, who also spoke עִבְרִית (*ivrit*), Hebrew, was someone who crossed over מֵעֵבֶר לַנָּהָר (*me'ever la-nahar*), from the other side of the [Euphrates] River. All these words—and more—use the root ע-ב-ר (*ayin, vet, resh*), to cross over a multitude of boundaries—geographical, economic and ethical.

In Scripture, the Prophet Jonah, asked to identify himself, proclaimed proudly, עִבְרִי אָנֹכִי (*ivri anokhi*), "I am a Hebrew." An *ivri* may also be one who sometimes עוֹבֵר עֲבֵרָה (*over avera*), commits a transgression against God, while God is one who עֹבֵר עַל פֶּשַׁע (*over al pesha*), overlooks sin. Imagine Moses' reaction when told לֹא תַעֲבֹר (*lo ta'avor*), "you shall not cross over" into the Promised Land. Abraham pays for his burial cave with כֶּסֶף עֹבֵר לַסֹּחֵר (*kesef over la-soher*), "money passing to the merchant," i.e., current currency. Balaam cannot curse the Israelites because, he admits, לֹא אוּכַל לַעֲבֹר (*lo ukhal la-avor*), "I cannot go beyond" God's wishes. For his famous wrestling match with the angel, Jacob crosses the מַעֲבַר יַבֹּק (*ma'avar yabbok*), Jabbok Ford. In the עָבָר (*avar*), past, on the day that became Passover, God announced וְעָבַרְתִּי (*ve-avarti*), "I shall pass through" Egypt for the 10th plague.

The rabbis insisted on personal responsibility by affirming that there is no such thing as an agent לִדְבַר עֲבֵרָה (*li-devar avera*), for a sinful act. A מַעְבֹּרֶת (*ma'aboret*) is both a ferryboat and the passage through which a *tefillin* strap is threaded. In the High Holy Day liturgy, we are told that repentance, prayer and *tzedaka* מַעֲבִירִין (*ma'avirin*), negate, the evil decree.

Let us now make an elegant מַעֲבָר (*ma'avar*), transition, to modern times with a reminder of the not-so-elegant מְעֻבָּרָה

(*ma'abara*), transit camp, through which early immigrants to Israel passed. At the obstetrician, the sonogram revealing an עֻבָּר (*ubbar*), embryo, confirms that the woman is מְעֻבֶּרֶת (*me'ubberet*), pregnant. Seven times in a 19-year cycle of the Jewish calendar we have a שָׁנָה מְעֻבֶּרֶת (*shana me'ubberet*), an extended year. Some believe that the expression עוֹבֵר וּבָטֵל (*over u-vatel*), senile, עוֹבֵר כָּל גְּבוּל (*over kol gevul*), goes beyond all bounds, of decency. In basketball lingo, an עֲבֵרָה לָתֵת (*avera la-tet*), literally, "foul to give," is the final foul before incurring a penalty shot.

When the radio operator on the battlefield ends his communication, he shortens the English expression "over and out" and מְעַבְרֵת (*me'avret*), Hebraizes it, crossing the language border with the word עֲבוֹר (*avor*), over!

Hebraizing is also what *Hebrew Matters* does. *Avor!*

68

Let It Stand

ע-מ-ד

ayin-mem-dalet

Have you ever noticed how hard it is to mean what you say? It is all the fault of idioms, where words take on metaphoric colorations remote from their original sense. Take, for example, the verb לְהַעֲמִיד (*le-ha'amid*), to cause to stand. Idiomatically, *Pirke Avot* promotes a version of open admissions, declaring הַעֲמִידוּ (*ha-amidu*), produce, many disciples. A leitmotif of novelist Ronit Matalon's *The One Facing Us* (Holt) is the heroine's concern that she not מַעֲמִיד פָּנִים (*ma'amid panim*), impart false airs. A chairman may decide לְהַעֲמִיד לְמִנְיָן (*le-ha'amid le-minyan*), to put an issue to a vote.

The root ע-מ-ד (*ayin, mem, dalet*) has an array of definitions, including both verbs and nouns: it can mean to stand, come forth, stand up, stand still, stop or continue.

In Scripture, the moon עָמַד (*amad*), stood still, for Joshua over the Valley of Ayalon. The daughters of Zelophehad תַּעֲמֹדְנָה (*ta'amodna*), stood, before Moses to petition him for their rightful inheritance. In a different key, after foremother Leah had borne Jacob four sons, וַתַּעֲמֹד מִלֶּדֶת (*va-ta'amod mi-ledet*), "she [temporarily] stopped bearing." As for nouns, Samson took hold of עַמּוּדֵי הַתָּוֶךְ (*ammudei ha-tavekh*), "the central pillars," and caused the Philistine temple to come crashing down.

Probably the most pregnant biblical use of our root is found in Leviticus, in the injunction לֹא תַעֲמֹד עַל דַּם רֵעֶךָ (*lo ta'amod al dam re'ekha*), "you shall not stand [idly] by the blood of your neighbor." The Talmud in tractate Sanhedrin, on page 73, עַמּוּד אָלֶף (*ammud alef*), the recto side, interprets that verse as an imperative to actively attempt to save someone who is being assaulted. Elsewhere in the Talmud, rabbinic lawmakers are directed not to issue a restrictive injunction that the general public is unable לַעֲמֹד בָּהּ (*la-amod ba*), to endure.

A transgressor was once placed in an עַמּוּד הַקָּלוֹן (*ammud ha-kalon*), pillory of shame. Today, a מֻעֲמָד (*mu'ammad*), candidate, for political office or for a job most likely comes from the middle מַעֲמָד (*ma'amad*), class, of society. Once the army takes a strategic עֶמְדָּה (*emda*), position, soldiers may be told עֲמוֹד נֹחַ (*amod no'ah*), "at ease," and they may be offered a container of חָלָב עָמִיד (*halav amid*), nonperishable milk. An עַמּוּד (*ammud*), lectern, is used as a stand on which to place one's Siddur while reciting the עֲמִידָה (*amida*), standing, *Shemoneh Esrei* prayer. Those who suffer backache will be painfully aware of their עַמּוּד הַשִּׁדְרָה (*ammud ha-shidra*), spinal column.

OK, נַעֲמוֹד כָּאן (*na'amod kan*), let's stop here, while we can still stand.

69

Still Waters Run *Amok*

ע-מ-ק
ayin-mem-kof

Have you ever noticed that, when trying to articulate deep thoughts, people often find it difficult to express themselves simply and clearly? In Hebrew, this is not strange: the root ע-מ-ק (*ayin, mem, khof*), to be deep, is itself used to describe unfathomable language. Perhaps that is why the biblical prophets Isaiah and Ezekiel both use עֹמֶק שָׂפָה (*omek safa*) to mean unintelligible speech. Leviticus uses the expression עָמֹק מֵעוֹר בְּשָׂרוֹ (*amok me-or besaro*), "deep from his skin's flesh," to refer to a leprous growth. Medieval Hebrew grammarian Jonah Ibn Janah deduces from these examples that the original meaning of the root is "distant"—distant from normal language or far from the natural look of skin.

According to Hebrew expert Reuven "Ruvik" Rosenthal, the word עֵמֶק (*emek*), valley, is a key word in the Zionist vocabulary. Emek Bet She'an (some 390 feet below sea level), Emek ha-Huleh (the famous swamp drained by early pioneers) and Emek Jezreel (a large fertile plain) are landmarks in the story of the settlement of Israel. The poet Nathan Alterman composed the lyrics (with music by Kurt Weill) of שִׁיר הָעֵמֶק (*shir ha-emek*), "Song of the Valley," inviting the weary pioneers in the Emek Jezreel to rest from their labors.

Although some scholars disagree, one might speculate that the place named עֵמֶק הַבָּכָא (*emek ha-bakha*), described in Psalms as a fertile spring-watered landscape, became—thanks to the similarity of בָּכָא (*bakha*), mulberry tree, to בָּכָא (*bakha*), weeping—a metaphorical "Vale of Tears." It refers variously to a cemetery, the diaspora and the suffering in this world. *Be-Emek ha-Bakha* is the Hebrew translation of a series of Yiddish short stories on Russian

Jewish life written by Mendele Mokher Seforim (nom de plume of S.Y. Abramovich).

The word הִתְעַמְּקוּת (*hitamkut*) is used for delving deeply into an issue. While עַמְקָן (*amkan*) signifies a deep thinker, the Talmud warns against being an עוּמְקָן (*umkan*), one who hides his thoughts from others.

Israeli television's Hebrew maven Avshalom Kor weaves a story in which he teaches that the name of the town Petah Tikva is related obliquely to our root. At first, the founders of the city saw in the desolate area an עֵמֶק עָכוֹר (*emek akhor*), barren valley. Following the words of the prophet Hosea, they vowed to turn *emek akhor* into פֶּתַח תִּקְוָה (*petah tikva*), an opening for hope.

Today, עֵמֶק רְפָאִים (*emek refaim*), the biblical Valley of the Giants, is the name of the main drag in the chichi neighborhood of Jerusalem's German Colony. And let us not forget עֵמֶק הַסִילִיקוֹן (*emek ha-silikon*), Silicon Valley, which helps us express deep thoughts simply. Or not.

70

Similar, Not Identical

ע-ר-ה

ayin-resh-heh

ebrew often uses similar roots with similar meanings, and
another chapter suggests that ע-ר-מ (*ayin, resh, mem*) might
be related to ע-ר-ה (*ayin, resh, heh*), both having to do with
nakedness. But similar is not identical, and therein lies a story. In
Genesis, a drunken Noah is shamed when his son witnesses עֶרְוַת אָבִיו
(*ervat aviv*), "his father's nakedness." The holiness code of
Leviticus issues a dozen sexual prohibitions following the same
pattern: עֶרְוַת אָבִיךָ לֹא תְגַלֵּה (*ervat avikha lo tegalleh*), "You shall not
uncover the nakedness of your father" (mother, aunt, etc.). These
euphemisms refer to illicit sexual concourse with blood relations, in
which case resulting offspring are halakhically considered bastards.
The root curls into metaphor in the story of Egyptian vizier Joseph
who accuses his brothers of having come to spy on עֶרְוַת הָאָרֶץ (*ervat
ha-aretz*), "the land's [protected and therefore] naked places."

In the Talmud, the root raises gender issues that smack of
apologetics. When the Talmud says that a woman's voice is עֶרְוָה
(*ervah*), indecency, it implies only, we are told, that a man may not
say the Shema while a woman is singing nearby.

Taking a completely different semantic route, *ayin, resh,
heh*, to pour out, describes foremother Rebekah's graciousness
bestowed on Isaac's matchmaking servant. While watering her
visitor's camels, וַתְּעַר כַּדָּהּ (*va-te'ar kaddah*), Rebekah "poured her
jar" into the trough, then ran to refill her vessel. This sense is also
found in an edifying fundraising story in the book of Chronicles.
King Joash, in need of funds to cleanse the "House of the Lord"
defiled by Baal-worshiping Queen Athalia, imposes a benign tax to
be deposited in a strategically placed chest. When it is filled, וִיעָרוּ
אֶת הָאָרוֹן (*vi'aru et ha-aron*), the king's men emptied out the chest
and paid the contractors their due. When Lamentations chastises

inebriates and warns תִּתְעָרִי (*titari*), this means to one medieval commentator that, lewdness following hard on drunkenness, "You will run around naked." Another commentator will prefer a different explication: "You will [pour out] vomit," as drunks, he says, are wont to do.

Today, one encounters a spectrum of meanings: a מְעָרָה (*me'arah*), cave, is an empty space; shaving—making the face naked—entails a תַּעַר (*ta'ar*), straight razor; an עֲרוּי דָם (*eru'i dam*), transfusion, implies pouring blood into veins.

Does הֶעָרַת שׁוּלַיִים (*he'arat shulayyim*), footnote, also derive from our root? At the Hebrew University of Jerusalem library, where Academy Award contender *Footnote* was filmed, you'll find another possibility, as the shoresh for *he'arah*, note, ע-ו-ר (*ayin, vav, resh*), to clarify. Similar, but not identical, as always.

71

Piling On

ע-ר-מ

ayin-resh-mem

What is one to make of Hebrew when it takes one root and piles onto it half a dozen seemingly unrelated meanings? Is it a matter of linguistic poverty? Or is it rather a demonstration of cultural and linguistic flexibility? Take the case of ע-ר-מ (*ayin, resh, mem*), which, as an adjective, sometimes means deceitful, sometimes prudent and sometimes just plain naked. Used as a noun, it can describe a tree and its fruit, a bodily organ, a percussion instrument or a piled-up heap.

Think back to the story of Adam, Eve and the Serpent in the Garden of Eden. There, the root is used to tell us that the serpent was עָרוּם (*arum*) "craftier [than any beast of the field]." Just a few verses away, readers are informed that Adam and Eve in Eden are עֲרוּמִּים (*arummim*), naked, before eating of the forbidden fruit. Afterward, the first couple themselves become aware—with a change in punctuation—that they are עֵירֻמִּים (*erummim*), naked. Playing metaphorically on this sense, Job, learning of the disasters that have befallen him, recognizes that since he has emerged עָרֹם (*arom*), naked, from his mother's womb, he can reconcile himself to dying "naked" of his wealth and family.

One of the most powerful images in the Bible—with a nod to Cecil B. DeMille—appears in Moses' Song of the Sea, depicting the walls of water that נֶעֶרְמוּ (*ne'ermu*), were gathered in heaps, to provide a dry path through which the Israelites might pass. Setting the stage for a crucial scene in the book of Ruth, Boaz comes down to the field to lie down in the corner of an עֲרֵמָה (*aremah*), pile [of harvested wheat].

A surprisingly helpful derivation of the Hebrew root is עַרְמוֹן (*armon*), chestnut tree. Ernest Klein's *Etymological Dictionary of the Hebrew Language* (Macmillan) tries to pull our עַרְמוֹנִים

(*armonim*), chestnuts, out of the fire by suggesting that our root refers to stripping bare the bark of a tree. Klein hints that this might account for the correlation between a chestnut tree and nudity. Nevertheless, if you have a good imagination, it is quite easy to visualize how *armon* might engender עַרְמוֹנִי (*armoni*), the reddish-brown color of the chestnut, and עַרְמוֹנִית (*armonit*), both chestnut-shaped castanets and the prostate gland.

In the end, however, we are left with לְשׁוֹן עֲרוּמִים (*leshon arummim*), a conversation that hints of hidden mysteries. In another chapter, we see if, in the richness of the Hebrew language, ע-ר-ה (*ayin, resh, heh*), a sister root for nakedness, can help us unravel this semantic *aremah*.

72

Living from Mouth to Mouth

פ-ה

peh-heh

Hebrew vocabulary often reflects the wisdom of the Hebrew nation. Take the example of the root פ-ה (*peh, heh*), giving us not only פֶּה (*peh*), mouth, but also a variety of proverbial sayings. If Hebrew is שָׁגוּר בְּפִיךָ (*shagur be-fikha*), fluent in your mouth, you will not wonder at the extensive use of the root. When God tells Moses to speak to Pharaoh, the reluctant prophet counters that he is כְּבַד פֶּה (*kevad peh*), "heavy of mouth," lacking in eloquence. And yet, only with Moses does God speak directly, פֶּה אֶל פֶּה (*peh el peh*), mouth to mouth. When a previous Pharaoh, appointing Joseph vizier, reassures him עַל פִּיךָ יִשַּׁק כָּל עַמִּי (*al pikha yishak kol ami*), he does not mean, "My entire nation shall kiss you on the mouth." Rather, they will do Joseph's bidding.

Jewish law decides cases עַל פִּי שְׁנַיִם עֵדִים (*al pi shenayim edim*), based on the testimony of two witnesses; sometimes, the fine is פִּי שְׁנַיִם (*pi shenayim*), double.

Were you aware that rabbinic Judaism begins in the mouth? That's where we find the expression תּוֹרָה שֶׁבְּעַל פֶּה (*torah she-be'al peh*), Oral Law. The rabbis asserted that the first two of the Ten Commandments were spoken directly by God, מִפִּי הַגְּבוּרָה (*mi-pi ha-gevura*), from the mouth of Power. A rabbinic proverb, using the Aramaic form of the root, reassures the industrious worker לְפוּם צַעֲרָא אַגְרָא (*le-fum tsa'ara agra*), the reward is commensurate with the pains taken. Modern Hebrew likes the Aramaic version, too. From פּוּם (*pum*), mouth, we derive פּוּמִית (*pumit*), cigarette holder or the mouthpiece of a telephone or saxophone.

If you're worried about self-fulfilling prophecies, אַל תִּפְתַּח פֶּה לַשָּׂטָן (*al tiftah peh la-satan*), don't make an opening for the devil to come in. An outrageous statement is countered with יִשְׁמְעוּ אָזְנֶיךָ מַה שֶׁפִּיךָ מְדַבֵּר (*yishme'u oznekha ma she-pikha medabber*), let your ears hear what your mouth is saying. Insincerity is אֶחָד בַּפֶּה וְאֶחָד בַּלֵּב (*ehad ba-peh ve-ehad ba-lev*), one thing in the mouth and quite another in the heart.

Because many publishers are careful not to use נִבּוּל פֶּה (*nibbul peh*), vulgar language, we will not emphasize the expression סְתוֹם אֶת הַפֶּה (*setom et ha-peh*), shut your mouth!

We say this בַּחֲצִי פֶּה (*ba-hatsi peh*), with half a mouth, i.e., hesitatingly, but many an Israeli politician, though blessed with פִּתְחוֹן פֶּה (*pithon peh*), eloquence, is a פֶּה גָּדוֹל (*peh gadol*), big mouth. Nevertheless, אַף עַל פִּי כֵן (*af al pi khen*), rarely will you hear that a measure in the Knesset was passed פֶּה אֶחָד (*peh ehad*), unanimously. For lovers of democracy, this is also wisdom.

73

Good-bye and Good Riddance

פ-ט-ר

peh-tet-resh

There are two types of people in this world: those who leave without saying good-bye and those who say good-bye but never seem to leave. The Hebrew root פ-ט-ר (*peh, tet, resh*), to take leave, demonstrates that leaving is somewhat more complex than that. Originally, the root meant to break open, as in the biblical expression פֶּטֶר רֶחֶם (*peter rehem*), first issue of the womb, a mother's firstborn child. The psalmist feels mocked; all who see him, he says, יַפְטִירוּ בְשָׂפָה (*yaftiru ve-safa*), "let curses break through their mouths." In the story of young David's unpleasant dealings with his father-in-law, we are told, וַיִּפָּטֵר מִפְּנֵי שָׁאוּל (*va-yiftar mipnei sha'ul*), "he fled from Saul."

The rabbis used our root especially as it pertains to the leave-taking known as divorce, pointing out that correct pronunciation is crucial in such matters. A husband saying פְּטָרוּהָ (*pitruha*) could be declaring nothing more than "release her from debt"; one who says פַּטְרוּהָ (*patruha*) means "release her from the marriage" by preparing a גֵּט פִּטּוּרִין (*get piturin*), bill of divorce.

And what about the weekly *haftara*, which stems from our root? The noun הַפְטָרָה (*haftara*) is related to the verb הִפְטִיר (*hiftir*), which means to adjourn a meeting or to recite something prior to the adjournment. The מַפְטִיר (*maftir*) is called to the Torah to recite the closing text, thereby "dismissing" us from the public reading. At a bar mitzva ceremony, the boy's father recites בָּרוּךְ שֶׁפְּטָרַנִי (*barukh she-petarani*), the blessing that indicates that the father is exempt from legal responsibility for his son's behavior. Today, *barukh she-petarani* is used colloquially to mean good riddance.

We are all painfully aware that dying is a radical form of leave-taking. Hebrew accounts for this nuance in the nouns פְּטִירָה (*petira*), death, and נִפְטָר (*niftar*), the deceased. Since death and taxes often go together, you'll be glad to hear that some products are פְּטוּרִים מִמַּס (*peturim mi-mas*), tax-exempt. We all know someone who is always seeking a פְּטוֹר (*petor*), exemption, from a requirement. Listen carefully when your friend tells you she no longer has a job: Did she say הִתְפַּטַרְתִּי (*hitpatarti*), I resigned, or הִתְפּוּטַרְתִּי (*hitputarti*), I was forced to resign? One command soldiers don't mind hearing is פְּטוּרִים (*peturim*), dismissed!

Some lexicographers believe that the word פִּטְרִיָּה (*pitriyya*), mushroom, comes from our root, perhaps because some mushrooms are poisonous and can cause the ultimate leave-taking. But then there is the other type of language maven, who simply takes leave by concluding abruptly.

74

Much Ado About Doing

פ-ע-ל

peh-ayin-lamed

Jean-Paul Sartre, in his existentialist play *No Exit*, posits that what you have actually done—not what you have been—is what defines your life. In Hebrew, there is a verb for that—פָּעַל (*pa'al*), to do. The three letters of the root, פ-ע-ל (*peh, ayin, lamed*), to make, achieve, accomplish, were chosen by medieval Hebrew grammarian Dunash Ibn Labrat as the paradigm for all פְּעָלִים (*pe'alim*), verbs. (That Dunash did not go with ק-ט-ל [*kof, tet, lamed*], to kill, which has properties that other grammarians might have preferred, tells a great deal about Jewish sensitivity to the power of words.)

In Scripture, the root is ascribed to God, of whom it says, תָּמִים פָּעֳלוֹ (*tamim pa-alo*), "His actions are righteous." In the rabbinic midrash on Psalms, God is quoted as saying בְּשֵׁשֶׁת פָּעַלְתִּי אֶת הָעוֹלָם (*be-sheshet pa'alti et ha-olam*), "In six days I made the world." In *Pirke Avot*, reminding us that the day is short and the work substantial, the sages grumble that הַפּוֹעֲלִים עֲצֵלִים (*ha-po'alim atselim*) the workers are lazy.

Our root is not at all lazy. It is so energetic that it does the work of several English words. In the apiary, where there are no male *po'alim*, there are many female פּוֹעֲלוֹת (*po'alot*), worker bees. A radio drama may use various פַּעֲלוּלִים (*pa'alulim*), sound effects, to good effect. An action that is correct *be-khoah*, in theory, is not necessarily so בְּפוֹעַל (*be-fo'al*), in practice. If a מְנַהֵל בְּפוֹעַל (*menahel be-fo'al*), acting manager, hires a פּוֹעֵל יוֹמִי (*po'el yomi*), day laborer, he must be careful not to withhold, even overnight, the worker's פְּעוּלַת שָׂכִיר (*pe'ulat sahir*), wages. And אַל תִּתְפָּעֵל (*al titpa'el*), do not be astonished, that the players on the Hapoel Tel Aviv soccer team are well compensated.

If you are רַבַּת פְּעָלִים (*rabbat pe'alim*), very energetic, and פְּעִילָה (*pe'ilah*), diligent, and wish לְהוֹצִיא לְפוֹעַל (*le-hotsi la-po'al*), to accomplish, a certain פּוֹעַל יוֹצֵא (*po'al yotse*), end result, you don't necessarily have to belong to the וַעַד הַפּוֹעַל (*va'ad ha-po'el*), executive committee. Of course, if you hold a winning ticket from the מִפְעַל הַפַּיִס (*mif'al ha-payis*), National Lottery, you can do anything you want.

Do not forget, however, that grandma's second gift for the newborn—after the hefty Israel Bond—should be a פַּעֲלוּלוֹן (*pa'alulon*), the toy gym that hangs above the stroller and encourages babies to exercise their senses of touch, sound and sight. The point here is to condition the child's brain to realize that פְּעִילוּת (*pe'ilut*), doing, is the essence of being.

75

Lub-Dub, Lub-Dub

פ-ע-מ

peh-ayin-mem

How is Hebrew reminiscent of the first moonwalk? The language's small steps also turn into giant strides. Take the example of פַּעַם (*pa'am*, accent on the first syllable), an onomatopoetic word—if one listens carefully—for footfall, used widely today for counting the times something occurs. The root פ-ע-מ (*peh, ayin, mem*), to strike, gives birth to a wide spectrum of meanings in Scripture. From a footfall to a beautifully advancing shod foot is a small step in the Song of Songs, where the beloved is praised מַה יָּפוּ פְעָמַיִךְ בַּנְעָלִים (*ma yafu pe'amayikh ba-ne'al-im*), "How beautiful are your sandaled footsteps." Another small step takes us to fear of the unknown. When Pharaoh awoke from his enigmatic dreams, וַתִּפָּעֶם רוּחוֹ (*va-tipa'em ruho*), "his spirit was agitated." Judges keeps pace when it tells us the exact circumstances of Samson's first steps into prophecy, וַתָּחֶל רוּחַ ה' לְפַעֲמוֹ (*va-tahel ru'ah ha-shem le-fa'amo*), "The spirit of the Lord began to move him." A *pa'am* is also a way of counting units. Think of Moses, who makes a big misstep—causing gushes of water and Godly wrath—when he hits the rock פַּעֲמָיִם (*pa'amayim*), twice.

It does not take too much imagination to see how פַּעֲמוֹן (*pa'amon*), bell—an instrument in which a clapper strikes a piece of metal—comes from our root. The best-known bell in the Torah is part of the פַּעֲמֹן וְרִמֹּן (*pa'amon ve-rimmon*), bell and pomegranate, that are sewn on the high priest's robe. Lexicographers disagree on the Hebrew word for glockenspiel calling it, variously, פַּעֲמוֹנָה (*pa'amona*), פַּעֲמוֹנִיָּה (*pa'amoniyya*) or פַּעֲמוֹנֶת (*pa'amonet*). At least they agree on פַּעֲמוֹנָר (*pa'amonar*), bell ringer. According to Ruth Almagor-Ramon, writer of *A Moment of Hebrew* radio spots, the Hebrew Language Academy has accepted פַּעֲמָן (*pa'aman*) for metronome.

You'll find our root in a bevy of modern idioms. An Israeli restaurant advertises that it has הַטַּעַם שֶׁל פַּעַם (*ha-ta'am shel pa'am*), the taste of long ago. Sometimes, לִפְעָמִים (*lif'amim*), you'll hear someone bellow פַּעַם אַחַת וּלְתָמִיד (*pa'am ahat u-le-tamid*), once and for all. A one-time offer is חַד-פַּעֲמִי (*had-pa'ami*). An invitation to come and visit can be made by saying קְפוֹץ פַּעַם (*kefots pa'am*), jump over one time. In medicine, הַדּוֹפֶק פּוֹעֵם (*ha-dofek po'em*), the pulse beats. In poetry, לִבִּי פּוֹעֵם (*libi po'em*), my heart beats.

The Hebrew equivalent of "once in a blue moon," פַּעַם בְּיוֹבֵל (*pa'am be-yovel*), once in a 50-year cycle, comes to us from the Jewish tradition where, אֵי-פַּעַם (*ei-pa'am*), once, we celebrated the Jubilee year. Perhaps Neil Armstrong—because he's been there—can tell us how long a blue moon lasts.

76

Divide and Conquer

פ-ר-ד

peh-resh-dalet

A t times, one cannot help but marvel at the flexibility of Hebrew's three-letter roots as they fashion themselves into a wondrous variety of meanings. Take the root פ-ר-ד (*peh, resh, dalet*), to separate, which gives us—among others—mules, a choosing game, signs of God's love and marital problems. The root is found in some of the most famous phrases in Scripture. After Noah's flood, נִפְרְדוּ הַגּוֹיִם (*nifredu ha-goyim*), "the nations of the world split off." Abram, frustrated with his nephew Lot's poaching, proposes, הִפָּרֶד נָא מֵעָלַי (*hippared na me-alai*), "Please separate from me." A loyal Ruth tells her mother-in-law, Naomi, that only death יַפְרִיד בֵּינִי וּבֵינֵךְ (*yafrid beini u-veineikh*), "shall part me from you." And villainous Haman "accuses" the Jewish nation of being מְפֹרָד בֵּין הָעַמִּים (*meforad bein ha-ammim*), "scattered among the nations."

On another register, King David, to underline his choice of Solomon as his successor, orders that his son ride עַל הַפִּרְדָּה אֲשֶׁר לִי (*al ha-pirda asher li*), "on my mule." What is the connection between mules and our root? Hai Ga'on (d. 1038) explains that because a mule doesn't procreate, it is נִפְרָד (*nifrad*), separate, one of a kind. When the prophet Hosea scolds those who עִם הַזֹּנוֹת יְפָרֵדוּ (*im ha-zonot yeparedu*), "go off with prostitutes," some commentators suggest that contraception is being used here, so that this act, as with the mules of our root, will not produce offspring.

Since the Torah does not fully explain the existence of Shemini Atzeret, the day added on to the seven days of Sukkot, the midrash explains that, like a lover who does not wish his beloved to leave, God asks the Israelites to tarry one more day, because קָשָׁה עָלַי פְּרֵדַתְכֶם (*kashah alai peredatkhem*), "Your departure is a hardship for me."

In 1985, Israeli playwright Hillel Mittelpunkt staged a drama about marital discord called פֵּרוּד זְמַנִי (*perud zemani*), *Temporary Separation*. And a 2009 Oscar-winning Japanese film called, in Hebrew, פְּרֵדוֹת (*peredot*), *Departures*, portrays the preparation of the "dear departed" for the next world.

A *pered* is also a single dried pomegranate seed. Choosing "odds or evens" is called, in Hebrew, זוּג אוֹ פֶּרֶד (*zug o pered*), literally, "pair or one." Today, a נֶשֶׁף פְּרֵדָה (*neshef peredah*) is a going-away party. Scientists in the lab deal with פְּרוּדוֹת (*perudot*), molecules. To solve difficult algorithm problems by breaking them into sub-problems, Hebrew-speaking IT experts use a method called הַפְרֵד וּמְשׁוֹל (*hafred u-meshol*), divide and conquer. Roman conqueror Julius Caesar would have been amazed at this Hebrew vocabulary development.

77

Small Details

פ-ר-ט

peh-resh-tet

W hat do a grape, a guitar pick and a penny have in common? To begin with, they're all relatively small. In addition, in Hebrew, they all derive from פ-ר-ט (*peh, resh, tet*), to break apart, a root that appears twice in Scripture. Leviticus places the root in the sphere of Jewish ethics. At harvest time, when individual grapes fall to the ground they must be left in the fields for poor people and "strangers" to glean, as it is written, וּפֶרֶט כַּרְמְךָ לֹא תְלַקֵּט (*u-feret karmekha lo telaket*), "Neither shall you gather the scattered grapes of your vineyard." The prophet Amos chastises those who, a little too "at ease in Zion," do not have the general welfare in mind. These, he admonishes, lie on ivory beds, feast on lambs and פֹּרְטִים עַל פִּי הַנָּבֶל (*portim al pi ha-navel*), "strum upon the harp."

The rabbis of the talmudic era used the verb *portim* as a noun, for musicians in general. Whimsically, perhaps, according to medieval grammarian David Kimchi (Radak), they derived it from the פְּרוּטָה (*peruta*), small coin, that, they said, people would give to the performers. The modern noun מַפְרֵט (*mafret*), guitar pick, is derived from the word for plucking on the strings of an instrument.

The rabbis declared that when a person passes from the world, כָּל מַעֲשָׂיו נִפְרָטִים לְפָנָיו (*kol ma'asav nifratim lefanav*), all his deeds pass before him—one by one. Putting on a fringed garment, *tsitsit*, one recites a rabbinic formula: the mitzva has been accomplished בְּכָל פְּרָטֶיהָ (*bekhol perateha*), "in all its details." Jewish law is often מְפֹרָט (*meforat*), explicit and detailed, but it also depends on how the כְּלָל וּפְרָט (*kelal u-ferat*), the general and the particular, are laid out in a text.

There is a good deal of concern these days about confidentiality on the web, בִּפְרָט (*biferat*), in particular, about פְּרָטִיּוּת בְּפֵייסְבּוּק (*pratiyut be-fesbuk*), Facebook privacy. Today, when you go to a restaurant the waiter will hand you an itemized תַּפְרִיט (*tafrit*), menu. Food labels will provide a פֵּרוּט (*pirut*), listing of nutritional value. And when you need לִפְרוֹט (*lifrot*), to "break," a large bill, you go to the bank, which is open every day, פְּרָט לְשַׁבָּת (*perat le-shabbat*), except for Shabbat.

Some people, impatient with פְּרָטִים קְטַנִּים (*peratim ketanim*), small, seemingly unimportant details, believe that אֵין צוֹרֶךְ לְפָרֵט כָּל כַּךְ (*ein tsorekh le-faret kol kakh*), there's no need to go into such detail. But if you wish to compose a פֶּרֶט מִלִּים (*peret millim*), vocabulary list, that's surely the way to go.

78

To the Woodshed, Hebrew Style

פ-ר-ק

peh-resh-kof

I n English, one way to teach a wayward son a lesson is to "take him to the woodshed" for a thrashing. In Hebrew, one says אֲנִי אֲלַמֵּד אוֹתוֹ פֶּרֶק (*ani alammed oto perek*), "I will teach him a lesson." The use here of the word פֶּרֶק (*perek*), chapter, teaches a lesson not only to wayward sons but also to lovers of Hebrew. The noun derives from a verbal root, פ-ר-ק (*peh, resh, kof*), that originally meant to break into parts.

The root is used sparingly in Scripture. In Genesis, Isaac promises his son Esau וּפָרַקְתָּ עֻלּוֹ (*u-farakta ullo*), "you shall break Jacob's yoke [from your neck]." In I Kings, a strong wind מְפָרֵק הָרִים (*mefarek harim*), "splits the mountains," before Elijah's eyes. Obadiah uses the noun form to warn the House of Esau אַל תַּעֲמֹד עַל הַפֶּרֶק (*al ta'amod al ha-perek*), "do not stand at the crossroads [to do violence]."

The rabbis love our root and use it copiously. Most prominent are פִּרְקֵי אָבוֹת (*Pirke Avot*), Chapters of the Fathers; in Aramaic, the prayer יְקוּם פֻּרְקָן (*yekum purkan*), "May salvation"—i.e., lifting the burden—"come" from heaven; and the line in the Shabbat hymn, "*Yah Ribbon*", פְּרוֹק יַת עָנָךְ (*perok yat anakh*), "save your flock" from the mouth of the lions. In the High Holiday liturgy, the ideal cantor is described as פִּרְקוֹ נָאֶה (*pirko na'eh*), arrived at a pleasing stage in life.

In Modern Hebrew, the expression עַל הַפֶּרֶק (*al ha-perek*) means on the agenda. Before beginning to write, one draws up רָאשֵׁי פְּרָקִים (*rashei perakim*), an outline of major headings. When you say הִיא יוֹדַעַת פֶּרֶק (*hi yoda'at perek*), you're talking of a woman who knows her stuff. A longshoreman spends his days in פְּרִיקָה (*perika*), unloading cargo. A soldier is taught פֵּרוּק (*peruk*), how to break down a rifle, which is hard to do if you have sore מִפְרָקִים (*mifrakim*), joints.

In math, you can break down a number by פְּרִיקוּת (*perikut*), factoring. The founding of Israel פָּתַח פֶּרֶק חָדָשׁ (*patah perek hadash*), began a new chapter in the annals of Jewish history.

One of the solemn synonyms for the Qur'an is *al-Furkan*, which comes from our root via an Arabic word like the Aramaic word for salvation. And then there is King Farouk, whose name goes back to the 7th century. According to Islamic tradition, Caliph Umar Ibn al-Khattab was called *al-Parouk* by Mohammed because he was skilled at separating the good from the bad.

At the end of this *perek*, one must admit that, לִפְרָקִים (*lifrakim*), from time to time, it's good to be taught a lesson—the woodshed notwithstanding.

79

Mene Mene Tekel U-Farsin

פ-שׁ-ר

peh-shin-resh

T he book of Daniel suggests that when Belshazzar, king of
Babylon, sees a disembodied hand writing on the palace wall,
it is already too late. His fate is doubly sealed when the
prophet Daniel is called in to פִּשְׁרֵהּ (*fishreh*), in Aramaic, interpret,
the graffiti. Daniel forthrightly tells the king of his imminent doom.
Most scholars agree the Hebrew root פ-שׁ-ר (*peh, shin, resh*), to
interpret, is borrowed from the Aramaic. It appears only once in
Hebrew Scripture—when Kohelet asks rhetorically for the פֵּשֶׁר
(*pesher*), meaning, of an adage. But the root has many more
meanings than "to tell the meaning." It can be traced back to the verb
פָּשַׁר (*pashar*), to melt or dissolve. Thus, the melting of ice between
winter and spring is called the פָּשִׁיר (*pashir*), melting season. Water
that is neither cold nor hot is מַיִם פּוֹשְׁרִים (*mayyim poshrim*),
lukewarm water. One who blows neither hot nor cold is a פּוֹשֵׁר
(*posher*), indifferent person.

So how do we get to the current meaning? When ice gets
dissolved, it turns into a "solution." From that to פֵּשֶׁר (*pesher*),
solution of a problem or riddle, requires only a medium-sized leap
of faith. A problem that is threatening to boil over is solved by hiring
a פַּשְׁרָן (*pashran*), mediator, and arriving at a פְּשָׁרָה (*peshara*),
compromise. So pleased were the rabbis with the spirit of
compromise that they insisted יָפֶה כֹּחַ הַפְּשָׁרָה (*yafeh ko'ah
ha-peshara*), preferable is the power of compromise, even to the
power of law. Compromise would be welcome in the discussion
among lexicographers on whether the word אֶפְשָׁר (*efshar*), possible,
is related to our root. Some say בִּלְתִּי אֶפְשָׁרִי (*bilti efshari*), impossible,
while others suggest it is a distinct אֶפְשָׁרוּת (*efsharut*), possibility.
The word *efshar* is found in many slang expressions. To put down a
self-important person, just ask אֶפְשָׁר לָגַעַת בְּךָ (*efshar la-ga'at bekha*),

may I touch you? To praise another's modest wisdom, you say אֶפְשָׁר
לְדַבֵּר אִתּוֹ (*efshar le-dabber itto*), he is someone worth talking to.
Israeli poet Natan Yonatan gets a little romantic when he writes that
"both love and light" אִי אֶפְשָׁר לֶאֱגוֹר (*i-efshar la-agor*), "are
impossible to store up."

Speaking of artists, if you would like to see Rembrandt's
painting of the Daniel story, Google "Belshazzar's Feast" and click
on the link to the National Gallery in London. With the help of this
chapter's title, see if you can find Rembrandt's typo.

80

Windows 1.0

צ-ה-ר

tsadi-heh-resh

W hat do you get when you combine theology with meteorology? During the fall, you get the biblical story of Noah's ark. You also get a fascinating Hebrew vocabulary lesson.To begin at the beginning, Scripture tells us that Noah's ark had two windows: one, the חַלוֹן (*halon*), through which Noah sent a dove to ascertain weather conditions; and the other, a צֹהַר (*tsohar*), an opening for daylight to enter the ark. Among its other meanings, the root צ-ה-ר (*tsadi, heh, resh*) denotes "to shine brilliantly." And so, the Talmud suggests that Noah's *tsohar* was a radiant gemstone, used to illuminate the ark.

In another derivation, Deuteronomy promises farmers who observe the commandments a bountiful crop of glistening יִצְהָר (*yits'har*), pure olive oil. Since oil is used in anointment ceremonies, the prophet Zechariah refers to a king and a high priest, both newly ordained, as שְׁנֵי בְנֵי הַיִּצְהָר (*shenei benei ha-yits'har*), literally, "two sons of olive oil." Today, the phrase is applied to honorable people.

The first formal luncheon in the Bible takes place in Egypt when Joseph informs his steward "these men [his brothers] will lunch with me" בַּצָּהֳרַיִם (*ba-tsohorayim*), "at noon." The word *tsohorayim* is correctly pronounced thus, and so is *tsahorayim*, according to television personality and Hebrew maven Avshalom Kor, the Sefardic pronunciation, but never *tsaharayim*. The word is used in casual speech as a synonym for lunch. Some restaurant ads play on the cordial greeting צָהֳרַיִם טוֹבִים (*tsohorayim tovim*), "Good afternoon," to invite prospective clients in for a "Good lunch." At midday, you will see restaurant menus announcing אֲרוּחַת צָהֳרַיִם עִסְקִית (*aruhat tsohorayim iskit*), business lunch. Speculating on why *tsohorayim* is written with the pairing suffix—*ayim*, as though it referred to a "double light"—medieval etymologist David Kimchi

(Radak) suggests this is so because the world receives its midday light simultaneously from two "*tsohars*": immediately before and after noon.

The coinage of הַצְהָרָה (*hats'harah*), declaration, by Eliezer Ben-Yehuda from לְהַצְהִיר (*le-hats'hir*), to declare, became widespread after 1917, with הַצְהָרַת בַּלְפוּר (*hats'harat balfur*), The Balfour Declaration. This use of the root is also found in legal documents such as תַּצְהִיר (*tats'hir*), product warranty or court deposition, and מִצְהָר (*mits'har*), cargo manifest. More widespread, the word צָהֲרוֹן (*tsa'haron*), refers to both an afternoon day care program and a newspaper published in the afternoon.

The most uplifting use of our root is found in the idiom בָּרוּר כַּשֶּׁמֶשׁ בַּצָּהֳרַיִם (*barur ka-shemesh ba-tsohorayim*), "as clear as the midday sun." You can find a variant of this expression on YouTube in Naomi Shemer's lively 1967 anthem "מָחָר" (*mahar*), "Tomorrow," where confidence in a bright future endures.

81

Defying Gravity

צ-ח-ק

tsadi-het-kof

We all know that he who laughs last laughs best. A look at the root צ-ח-ק (*tsadi, het, kof*), to laugh, reveals the significance of the first laughs in Jewish history. The announcement to Abraham and Sarah of the forthcoming birth of יִצְחָק (*yitshak*), Isaac, hints at the multiple meanings of the root. According to Rashi's commentary and Onkelos' translation of the biblical verses, Abraham's וַיִּצְחָק (*va-yitshak*) on hearing the news means he laughed joyfully, while Sarah's וַתִּצְחָק (*va-titshak*), means she laughed doubtfully. Sarah's embarrassment at bearing a child in old age is underlined when she asserts that God has played a צְחוֹק (*tsehok*), joke, on her and that anyone who hears of the birth יִצְחַק לִי (*yits'hak li*), "will make me a laughingstock."

When Lot tells his sons-in-law to escape Sodom before it is destroyed, they believe that he is כִּמְצַחֵק (*kimetsahek*), like one who jests. When Abimelekh looks out his window to see Isaac מְצַחֵק (*metsahek*), flirting, with Rebecca, the Philistine king realizes that Rebecca is Isaac's wife. When Moses tarries on Sinai to receive the Law, וַיָּקֻמוּ לְצַחֵק (*va-yakumu le-tsahek*), the Israelites "rose to dance" around the golden calf.

And then there is Ecclesiastes, who tells us there is a time to cry and a time לִשְׂחוֹק (*lis'hok*), to laugh. From this verse, and from the verse in Jeremiah that speaks of יִשְׂחָק (*yis'hak*) as a forefather, we learn that שׂ-ח-ק (*sin, het, kof*) is a collateral form of our root. Thus מִשְׂחָק (*mis'hak*) is a game, while, according to the Hebrew Language Academy, מִצְחָק (*mits'hak*) is stand-up comedy. It's enough to put a בַּת צְחוֹק (*bat tsehok*), smile, on your face. Also, while a שַׂחְקָן (*sahkan*) is an actor, a צַחְקָן (*tsahkan*) is someone who loves to laugh. In Modern Hebrew, you might say of a friend who has accomplished something with panache, הוּא שִׂחֵק אוֹתָהּ! (*hu sihek ota*), "He did great!"

Getting back to our original root, we encounter an edifying story of Rabbi Akiva. In 70 CE, when a group of rabbis come upon Jerusalem in ruins, all Akiva's companions cry; he laughs. They ask him, לָמָה אַתָּה מְצַחֵק? (*lama ata metsahek*), "Why are you laughing?" Akiva reminds them of the prophecy that after Jerusalem is destroyed, only then will redemption come. Hearing this, one might say, זֶה לֹא צְחוֹק (*zeh lo tsehok*), that's a serious story.

When someone takes a serious issue lightly, just say צְחוֹק, צְחוֹק (*tsehok, tsehok*), short for laugh all you want; you'll be sorry. When a Hebrew joke falls flat, the teller will often say, בְּאִידִישׁ זֶה מַצְחִיק מְאוֹד (*be-idish zeh mats'hik me'od*), in Yiddish it's very funny. Maybe the first laugh is better after all.

82

Smile, You're Reading
Candid Camera

צ-ל-מ
tsadi-lamed-mem

How do we know that language is central to one's identity?
Just look at the debates that have whirled around Hebrew:
Hebrew vs. Yiddish and German, Ashkenazi vs. Sefardi
pronunciation, to name a few. Even within Hebrew, words
themselves have been known to take sides. Look at the root צ-ל-מ
(*tsadi, lamed, mem*), which has both concrete and intangible
meanings: on the one hand, to carve out—as in statue; on the other,
to be dark—as in shadow.

The concrete sense is found in a verse in II Kings, וְאֶת צַלְמָיו
שִׁבְּרוּ (*ve-et tsalmav shibru*), "They smashed their idols." The
abstract meaning is found famously in the creation story, as God
announces, "Let us make man בְּצַלְמֵנוּ (*be-tsalmenu*), in our image."

In rabbinic literature, both senses can be found in the phrase
הֶעֱמִיד צֶלֶם בַּהֵיכָל (*he'emid tselem ba-heikhal*), literally, erected an idol
in the sanctuary; figuratively, defiled it. Today, we use the
expression בְּצֶלֶם אֱלֹקים (*be-tselem elokim*), "in God's image," to
remind ourselves to act virtuously. It is for this reason that an Israeli
human-rights organization calls itself *B'Tselem*.

A debate about one of the derivatives of our root has been
going on for centuries. It has to do with Psalm 23, recited at solemn
occasions. The verse "Yea though I walk through the valley of צַלְמָוֶת
(*tsalmavet*), I will fear no evil," leaves the reader with a conundrum.
The traditional translation of *tsalmavet* is "shadow of death," as
though it did not come from our root but from צֵל (*tsel*), shadow, and
מָוֶת (*mavet*), death. Modern scholars prefer to see *tsalmavet* as
deriving from our root. Noting that in Psalms the word *tsalmavet* is
paired with *hoshekh*, darkness—suggesting, by a method called

biblical parallelism, that they are synonyms—they translate the word as "deepest darkness."

In Modern Hebrew, the debate takes place in a darkroom. Educator David Yellin (1864–1941), seeking a word for photograph, went to the ancient root and carved out צֶלֶם (*tselem*), picture; צַלָּם (*tsalam*), photographer; and צַלְמָנִיָּה (*tsalmaniyya*), camera. Hayyim Nahman Bialik (1873–1934), not happy with Yellin's coinage for camera, came up with מַצְלֵמָה (*matslema*), an innovation that carried the day. All was not lost for Yellin, however. His *tsalmaniyya* survived in the expression for photographer's studio. Today, other words from our root help us to get the picture, for example, תַּצְלוּם (*tatslum*), photo, and צִלּוּם (*tsilum*), photocopy.

Next time you go לְהִצְטַלֵּם (*le-hitstallem*), to have your picture taken, don't forget that, even in those awful ID pictures, your image and God's are one.

83

Looking Forward

צ-פ-ה

tsadi-feh-heh

S eeing is believing, they say. Judaism asserts, as one of its 13 articles of faith, that believing implies an all-seeing Deity. In the *Yigdal* hymn, God צוֹפֶה וְיוֹדֵעַ סְתָרֵינוּ (*tsofeh ve-yo-de'a setareinu*), "looks out knowingly at our hidden acts." Derivations of the root צ-פ-ה (*tsadi, feh, heh*), to look out, are similarly far-ranging, going from prophesying to hoping to expecting and beyond.

In Scripture, Jacob and his father-in-law, Laban, part ways in such distrust that only the Lord יִצֶף (*yitsaf*), can assure their peaceful separation. The Woman of Valor צוֹפִיָּה הֲלִיכוֹת בֵּיתָהּ (*tsofiyya halikhot beita*), "monitors the activities of her household." King David turns despairingly to his צֹפֶה (*tsofeh*), watchman, for news of his beloved son Absalom. Lamentations describes the hopelessness of Jerusalem's inhabitants at the destruction of the First Temple, saying בְּצִפִּיָּתֵנוּ צִפִּינוּ (*be-tsipiyyateinu tsipinu*), "as we had hoped" for salvation from a foreign power, so we wait now in vain.

Prophecy is attached to our root in the Jerusalem Talmud, asserting that Moses צָפָה בְּרוּחַ הַקֹּדֶשׁ (*tsafa be-ru'ah ha-kodesh*), had visions in the spirit of holiness. The Talmud also relates that one question we will be asked on arrival in the world to come is צָפִּיתָ לִישׁוּעָה (*tsippita li-yeshu'a*), did you live in expectation of redemption? Then there is the nautical tale of Rabban Gamaliel's מְצוֹפִית (*metsofit*), viewing tube, through which he could gauge, for halakhic purposes, the distance from ship to shore. You needn't visit the city of Safed to know it is built on a hill. Just look for our root in its name, צְפַת (*tsefat*), a synonym for which is מִצְפֶּה (*mitspeh*), observation post.

Naftali Herz Imber, in "*Hatikva*," uses the root to assert עַיִן לְצִיּוֹן צוֹפִיָּה (*ayin le-tsiyyon tsofiyya*), our gaze is turned expectantly toward Zion. In the early 20th century in Warsaw, a visionary daily

Hebrew newspaper, הַצּוֹפֶה (*ha-tsofeh*), *The Observer*, published works by Hayyim Nahman Bialik and Mendele Mokher Sefarim. And Eliezer Ben-Yehuda coined a word that has gained military currency, תַּצְפִּית (*tatspit*), lookout post.

Scouts, צוֹפִים (*tsofim*), are trained for any eventuality. When we look back on our lives, some occurrences were בִּלְתִּי צְפוּיִּם (*bilti tsefuyyim*), unexpected, and others appear צָפוּיִּם מֵרֹאשׁ (*tsefuyyim me-rosh*), foreseeable. Today, the television announcer will wish her viewers צְפִיָּה מְהַנָּה (*tsefiya mehana*), pleasant viewing. A good צוֹפֶה (*tsofeh*), viewer, will see that the announcer מְצַפָּה לְתִּינוֹק (*metsappa le-tinnok*), is expecting a child. What could be more forward-looking than that?

84

The Immaculate Reception

ק-ב-ל

kof-bet-lamed

Thanks to its celebrity status, Kabbalah, the Jewish mystical tradition, has become a household word. Because of the hidden nature of its teachings, however, very few people understand what it is truly about. We do know that the Hebrew word קַבָּלָה (*kabbala*), Kabbalah, comes from the root ק-ב-ל (*kof, bet, lamed*), to receive or welcome, and that in addition to קַבָּלַת שַׁבָּת (*kabbalat shabbat*), the service to welcome Shabbat written by the Safed kabbalists, the word *kabbala* has a half-dozen meanings that have little to do with religion.

The original sense of the root is "to be opposite." Thus, Ezekiel uses the word קֹבֶל (*kovel*), "battering ram," to warn the residents of Tyre of their coming destruction. II Kings announces the public slaying of an evil ruler, קֳבָל-עָם (*kaval-am*), "before the people." The "opposite" sense is also found in the modern expression בְּמַקְבִּיל (*be-makbil*), in a parallel fashion. How do we get from there to here? Is it not מִתְקַבֵּל עַל הַדַּעַת (*mitkabbel al ha-da'at*), logical, that you would מְקַבֵּל (*mekabbel*), welcome, someone facing you?

At the end of the book of Esther, the Jews of Persia קִבְּלוּ עֲלֵיהֶם (*kibblu alei-hem*), "took it upon themselves"—and their descendants—to celebrate their victory. Earlier, Mordecai, dressed in sackcloth לֹא קִבֵּל (*lo kibbel*), "refused to accept," the more decorous clothing Esther sent him.

The primordiality of tradition in Jewish life is found prominently in *Pirke Avot*, which opens with מֹשֶׁה קִבֵּל תּוֹרָה מִסִּינַי (*moshe kibbel tora mi-sinai*), "Moses received the [oral] Torah at Sinai" and passed it on to subsequent generations, who accepted it in turn. *Pirke Avot* also uses the root to proclaim a basic principle of courtesy: הֱוֵי מְקַבֵּל אֶת כָּל הָאָדָם (*hevei mekabbel et kol ha-adam*),

"Greet everyone," with a cheerful countenance. The full Kaddish entreats, תִּתְקַבֵּל צְלוֹתְהוֹן (*titkabbel tsilotehon*), May our prayer be accepted.

Building a home? Hire a קַבְּלָן (*kabblan*), building contractor, who takes your task contractually upon himself. On the Internet, when you purchase a kabbalistic amulet, don't forget to ask for a קַבָּלָה (*kabbala*), receipt. Arriving at a hotel, you register at the קַבָּלָה (*kabbala*), reception desk. At a wedding, there is often a sumptuous קַבָּלַת פָּנִים (*kabbalat panim*), reception. Some marriages end less happily than they begin. A wife eager for a divorce may appoint a שָׁלִיחַ לְקַבָּלָה (*shaliah le-kabbala*), messenger authorized to receive a bill of divorce.

In Israeli slang, you might praise someone, jauntily saying יֵשׁ לוֹ קַבָּלוֹת (*yesh lo kabbalot*), he has corroborating documents—which means to say, he's the real thing. Can we say as much about our celebrity kabbalists?

85

Summertime, and the Living Is Grammatical

ק-י-צ

kof-yod-tsadi

O ver the centuries, Hebrew grammarians have looked for—and found—etymological connections between seemingly dissimilar derivations. Nevertheless, there are roots that resemble each other yet are unrelated. Take the example of the root ק-י-צ (*kof, yod, tsadi*), summer.

In Scripture, our root takes us to a climatological season, one of only two recognized in the ancient Near East. Psalm 74:17 acknowledges God's creation of these polarities: קַיִץ וָחֹרֶף אַתָּה יְצַרְתָּם (*kayits va-horef ata yetsartam*), "Summer and winter you created them."

The root also leads to an agricultural season, rolling out a generic word for summer fruit, קַיִצָה (*keitsa*). Specifically, the root refers to a fruit that ripens in summer—figs. The prophet Amos was by profession "a tender of sycamore fig trees." Fittingly, God's prophetic revelation to Amos involves the apparition of a כְּלוּב קַיִץ (*keluv kayits*), "basket of figs." Interpreting this vision, Amos, very much the doomsayer, cannot resist the temptation to make an etymologically chancy association between קַיִץ (*kayits*), summer, and קֵץ (*kets*), end. With these figs, he announces, בָּא הַקֵּץ אֶל עַמִּי (*ba ha-ketz el ammi*), "The end has come for my people."

Our root shows up in other Jewish texts: Proverbs 6:8 extols the industrious ant as if it were the Woman of Valor herself, saying תָּכִין בַּקַּיִץ לַחְמָה (*takhin ba-kayits lahmah*), "She lays up her stores during the summer." One of the less well-known episodes of Absalom's revolt against his father, King David, is an episode involving מֵאָה קַיִץ (*me'ah kayits*), "100 cakes of figs," as a bribe made to David on the battlefield. Apparently, David was not fond of Fig Newtons, since this effort at enticement did not work.

Today, students wishing to take a Hebrew immersion course register at a בֵּית סֵפֶר קַיִץ (*beit sefer kayits*), summer school. As Israel turns on its שְׁעוֹן קַיִץ (*she'on kayits*), summer clock, to give its residents an extra hour of sunshine, one can observe many fashionable women on Tel Aviv boulevards sporting a שִׂמְלָה קֵיצִית (*simlah keitsit*), summer dress.

The Aramaic cognate of *kayits*, קַיְטָא (*kayta*), summertime, has assumed a prominent place in modern Hebrew. In current Hebrew, קֵיטָנָה (*kaitanah*) is a summer camp; קֵיטָנִים (*kaitanim*), summer vacationers; and עִיר קַיִט (*ir kayit*), resort town. These expressions, having arrived in Mandate Palestine in the early 20th century, have, like other new arrivals, comfortably assimilated into modern Israel.

86

Sometimes, Less Is Too Much

ק-ל-ל
kof-lamed-lamed

When Wall Street is bullish, gains are always good. In many areas of real life, however, there is a lot to be said for losing. Hebrew has a word or two to say about all types of lessening—some good, some bad—and many of them derived from the root ק-ל-ל (*kof, lamed, lamed*), to be light. Think of קָלַל (*kallal*), to be slight, in the בִּנְיָן קַל (*binyan kal*), a grammatical term for a verb's "simple" form.

In the Bible's flood story, Noah notices gleefully כִּי קַלּוּ הַמַּיִם (*ki kallu ha-mayim*), that the waters have receded. Equating lightness with swiftness, David, lamenting the deaths of King Saul and his beloved son Jonathan, tells us hyperbolically that מִנְּשָׁרִים קַלּוּ (*mi-nesharim kallu*), "They were swifter than eagles." The death of Asahel in Samuel is attributed to the fact that he was so קַל בְּרַגְלָיו (*kal be-raglav*), "fleet-footed," that he caught up with his killer.

If you've ever wondered about the expression "A word to the wise is sufficient," look at the book of Proverbs, which uses our root in the expression דַעַת לְנָבוֹן נָקָל (*da'at le-navon nakal*), understanding comes "easily" to the wise.

Lexicographer Ernest Klein asserts that our root originally meant to belittle and was then applied to the verb קִלֵּל (*killel*), to curse. From this form are derived קְלָלָה (*kelalah*), malediction; קָלוֹן (*kalon*), degradation; and קִלְקֵל (*kelokel*), defective. The biblical punishment for one who מְקַלֵּל (*mekallel*), curses [his parents], is death. A blessing for the New Year is תִּכְלֶה שָׁנָה וְקִלְלוֹתֶיהָ (*tikhleh shanah ve-kileloteha*), may last year's curses, i.e., calamities, cease.

Rabbinic history reports that a lascivious prince was caught *in flagrante delicto*, בְּקַלְקָלָתוֹ (*be-kalkalato*), in a despicable seduction. Roman Emperor Vespasian is charged with disgracing

Judean nobles by shipping them to Roman בָּתֵי קָלוֹן (*batei kalon*), houses of disgrace, brothels.

The sages caution us to take seriously מִצְווֹת קַלּוֹת (*mitsvot kallot*), lightly-regarded precepts. Halakic argumentation will often use the hermeneutic device of קַל וָחוֹמֶר (*kal va-homer*), leading from a minor principle to a major one. The sage Hillel is considered an exemplary מֵקֵל (*mekel*), lenient judge, always seeking extenuating circumstances to issue a קֻלָּה (*kullah*), lenient ruling. The expression קַל שֶׁבַּקַּלִּים (*kal she-ba-kallim*), lightest of the light, is often reserved for intellectual lightweights who attain high office. Today, one will sometimes choose to eat an אֲרוּחָה קַלָּה (*aruhah kallah*), light snack, and drink מַשְׁקָאוֹת קַלִּים (*mashka'ot kallim*), soft drinks.

To judge by some Wall Street lifestyles, it doesn't hurt to lighten up a bit, לָקַחַת אֶת הַחַיִּים בְּקַלּוּת (*la-kahat et ha-hayyim be-kallut*), to take life easy.

87

Something Happened

ק-ר-ה

kof-resh-heh

D o things just happen? It's a theological question, to be sure, but also a Hebrew one. Rashi, the most famous of the biblical commentators, expounding on Leviticus 1:1, distinguishes between the homonymous verbs קָרָא (*kara*), he called, and קָרָה (*kara*), it happened. He posits that God actively seeks out his beloved prophet Moses, as the Torah illustrates using וַיִּקְרָא (*va-yikra*), "He called," but merely appears to the heathen prophet Balaam with וַיִּקָּר (*va-yikar*), "He happened upon."

The root ק-ר-ה (*kof, resh, heh*), to occur, does not always appear with such theological baggage. In the Joseph story, Jacob hesitates to send Benjamin down to Egypt, fearing וְקָרָהוּ אָסוֹן (*ve-karahu asson*), "lest he meet with an accident." In Exodus, Moses is told to announce to Pharaoh that the Hebrew God נִקְרָה עָלֵינוּ (*nikra aleinu*), "has manifested Himself to us." The dramatic tension of the book of Esther is heightened when the expression כָּל אֲשֶׁר קָרָהוּ (*kol asher karahu*), "all that happened to him," is used in connection with both Haman and Mordecai. The root is doubled in the expression וַיִּקֶר מִקְרֶהָ (*va-yiker mikreha*), "as luck would have it," to describe Ruth as she just happens to light precisely on the place where Boaz is lying. Ecclesiastes prefers the wise man to the fool but realizes that מִקְרֶה אֶחָד יִקְרֶה אֶת כֻּלָּם (*mikreh ehad yikreh et kulam*), "the same fate awaits them both."

The word קִרְיָה (*kirya*), city, is possibly related to our root—as a place where people happen to gather. It is found in such place names as קִרְיַת אַרְבַּע (*kiryat arba*), the early name for Hebron; קִרְיַת הָאוּנִיבֶרְסִיטָה (*kiryat ha-universita*), the university campus; and קִרְיַת הַוָּתִיקָן (*kiryat ha-vatikan*), Vatican City. In modern Israel, it is not בְּמִקְרֶה (*be-mikreh*), happenstance, that הַקִּרְיָה (*ha-kirya*), with the definite article, is used to denote the government center in Jerusalem.

A מִקְרֶה (*mikreh*) can be a neutral event that takes place, frequently or not, as in the expression בְּתִשְׁעָה מִקְרִים מְתוֹךְ עֲשָׂרָה (*be-tisha mikrim mi-tokh asara*), nine times out of ten. Or it can be an embarrassing accident, as in מִקְרֶה לַיְלָה (*mikreh laila*), nocturnal emission. Whether a job seeker thinks he may get an offer or not, it is good בְּכָל מִקְרֶה (*be-khol mikreh*), either way, to send in a קוֹרוֹת חַיִּים (*korot hayyim*), resume, literally, the events of one's life. When one shows up late for the interview because he had, also from our root, a תֶּקֶר (*teker*), flat tire, he will be asked מָה קָרָה (*ma kara*), what happened? And if he does not get the job? Let's face it, זֶה קוֹרֶה (*zeh koreh*), it happens.

88

Israel Bonds

ק-שׁ-ר

kof-shin-resh

S ome 25 years ago, when "About Hebrew" first appeared in *Hadassah Magazine*, its Hebrew title was בְּקֶשֶׁר לָעִבְרִית (*be-kesher la-ivrit*). Over the years—even as the column and the magazine evolved—the קֶשֶׁר (*kesher*), bond, to Hebrew has remained a קֶשֶׁר אָמִיץ (*kesher amitz*), strong bond.

   The root ק-שׁ-ר (*kof, shin, resh*), to bind, has also evolved. In Genesis, Judah explains, נַפְשׁוֹ קְשׁוּרָה בְנַפְשׁוֹ (*nafsho keshu-ra ve-nafsho*), Jacob's life is bound up with Benjamin's. To save their hostess Rahab from harm during the conquest of Canaan, Joshua's emissaries tell her: תִּקְשְׁרִי בַּחַלּוֹן (*tiksheri ba-halon*), "Tie [a red ribbon] on your window." In Deuteronomy, as the Israelites are about to cross into Canaan, God gives them a symbol to remind them of His commandments: וּקְשַׁרְתָּם לְאוֹת (*u-keshartam le-ot*), "You shall bind them as a sign." This symbol is the *tefillin* worn on the arm—the head strap being bound at the back by another *kesher*, a knot. Today, when we speak of knots in Israel, we think of Boy Scouts who, perhaps, tie a קֶשֶׁר סַבְתָּא (*kesher savta*), a not-too-complicated granny knot, or speedboats in Haifa's harbor that go עֶשְׂרִים קְשָׁרִים (*esrim kesharim*), 20 knots an hour.

   The root is found in a different הֶקְשֵׁר (*heksher*), context, in II Kings. There, *kesher* is not a bond, but a band of rebels who conspire to commit treason. When קוֹשְׁרִים (*koshrim*), conspirators, form an alliance to depose Queen Athalia, she wails קֶשֶׁר קֶשֶׁר (*kesher kesher*), "Conspiracy! Conspiracy!"

   One of the branches of the Army is חֵיל הַקֶּשֶׁר (*hel ha-kesher*), the signal corps, and a קַשָּׁר (*kashar*) is either a telegrapher or a liaison officer. A former Jerusalem bus cooperative, 1931–1967, with a deep historical *kesher* to Hadassah was named הַמְּקַשֵּׁר (*ha-mekasher*), "the linker." (The touchingly nostalgic website www.hamekasher.com has קִשּׁוּרִים [*kishurim*], Internet links, to the story of the 1948 Mount Scopus medical convoy massacre, in which several Hamekasher bus drivers were killed alongside Hadassah medical staff.)

Do not confuse Internet links with another up-to-date word: קְשָׁרִים (*kesharim*), business or political contacts. As they say, if you have good Israeli *kesharim*, you no longer need Russian-style *protektzia*.

Probably the most up-to-date form of our root is תִּקְשֹׁרֶת (*tikshoret*), telecommunications. The pervasiveness of this term not only permits us לְהִתְקַשֵּׁר (*le-hitkasher*), to contact one another at will, but has led to the creation of a new, four-letter root, ת-ק-שׁ-ר (*tav, kof, shin, resh*), to link up. More intimately, however, when taking leave, just say שְׁמוֹר עַל הַקֶּשֶׁר (*shemor al hakesh*)—keep in touch.

89

Much Ado About Plenty

ר-ב-ב
resh-vet-vet

Israeli elder statesman Shimon Peres liked to make the case that Israel, however lacking in natural resources, is nevertheless a land of plenty—of brains, that is. Hebrew is also a language of plenty, especially of words for plenty. Take, for example, the existence of not one, but two roots: ר-ב-ב (*resh, vet, vet*) and ר-ב-ה (*resh, vet, heh*), both of which mean to grow, to become great.

These roots are found widely in Scripture, beginning with the first mitzva in the Torah—פְּרוּ וּרְבוּ (*peru u-revu*), "Be fruitful and multiply." Leaving home, Rebekah receives a farewell blessing, "May you be לְאַלְפֵי רְבָבָה (*le-alfei revava*), the mother of myriads." In Exodus, Pharaoh wants to kill the Israelites' sons, פֶּן יִרְבֶּה (*pen yirbu*), "lest they multiply." And when the nation leaves Egypt, they are accompanied by an עֵרֶב רַב (*erev rav*), mixed multitude. David incurs Saul's wrath when the women sing a song comparing Saul's conquests of mere thousands with רִבְבֹתָיו (*rivevotav*), the young warrior's tens of thousands. Certain biblical rains are called רְבִיבִים (*revivim*), either because they are plentiful or because they grow abundant crops.

Is it any wonder that our רַבָּנִים (*rabbanim*), rabbis, had a predilection for this root, from which the word רַב (*rav*), rabbi, derives? They called God רִבּוֹנוֹ שֶׁל עוֹלָם (*Ribbono shel Olam*), Master of the Universe, and his prophet מֹשֶׁה רַבֵּנוּ (*Moshe Rabbeinu*), Moses our Teacher. When the rabbis said שְׂנָא אֶת הָרַבָּנוּת (*sena et ha-rabbanut*), they did not mean, literally, that one should hate the rabbinate, but rather that one should not try to become a public *macher*, (big shot, so called). The sage Hillel counsels, מַרְבֶּה נְכָסִים, מַרְבֶּה דְּאָגָה (*marbeh nekhassim, marbeh de'aga*), the more property you accumulate, the more worries you acquire.

Today, the root is no less רַבְגּוֹנִי (*ravgoni*), multifaceted. An important result of Zionism is רִבּוֹנוּת (*ribbonut*), sovereignty, i.e., self-mastery. When Elie Wiesel's *Night* was chosen for Oprah's Book Club, it immediately became a רַב-מֶכֶר (*rav-mekher*), best seller. When you want to tell someone "No!" in no uncertain terms, you say לֹא בְּאָלֶף רַבָּתִי (*lo be-alef rabbati*), no, with a capital *alef* (to distinguish לֹא from its homonym לוֹ [*lo*], which has no *alef* at all). Tel Aviv is a great city for תַּרְבּוּת (*tarbut*), culture, because to cultivate is to grow. And in תֵּל אָבִיב רַבָּתִי (*Tel Aviv rabbati*), Greater Tel Aviv—which you'd specify לְרַבּוֹת (*le-rabbot*), to include, the city's surrounding towns—you'll find plenty of the high-tech brains that Peres likes so much to talk about. Let's conclude therefore with תּוֹדָה רַבָּה (*toda rabba*), thanks a lot, to all of them—and all of you.

90

A Hundred More, with Feeling

ר-ג-שׁ
resh-gimel-shin

After 100 years of practical Zionism, members of Hadassah are well aware that there is an emotional component to their purposefulness. In Hebrew this is called, variously, רְגִישׁוּת (*regishuit*), sensitivity; רִגְשִׁיּוּת (*rigshiyyut*), sentimentality; and רַגְשָׁנוּת (*ragshanut*), emotionalism, and it has to do with a deeply felt affirmation of life itself.

While there are dozens of modern derivations of the root ר-ג-שׁ (*resh, gimel, shin*)—originally, to be in tumult; today, to feel—there are very few instances of the root in Scripture or rabbinic literature. There are verses in Psalms and the book of Daniel where the verbal form of the root means "to come in throngs" and where רֶגֶשׁ (*regesh*) is a noisy multitude. The midrash elucidates this usage by taking the phrase הוּא עָתִיד לְהַרְגִּישׁ (*hu atid le-hargish*) to mean "In the future, He will rouse and assemble [the nations in Jerusalem]."

Today, a *regesh* is an emotion and a רַגָּשׁ (*ragash*) is a sensitive person, while a רַגְשָׁן (*ragshan*) is often overly sentimental. When you hear someone exclaim, !בְּלִי רַגְשָׁנוּת (*beli ragshanut*), it is a plea to avoid sentimentalism. And yet, who does not enjoy an evening of שִׁירֵי מְדוּרָה רַגְשָׁנִיִּים (*shirei medurah ragshani'-im*), sentimental campfire songs? In a different key, singer Yossi Banai, channeling 20th-century French balladeer Georges Brassens, uses contemporary Hebrew slang to ask foremother Eve in heaven, אֵיךְ הַמַּרְגָּשׁ (*eikh ha-margash*), "How ya' doin'?"

When a classical pianist is רְגִישָׁה (*regisha*), sensitive, to her music, the critics will write that she played בְּרֶגֶשׁ (*be-regesh*), "with feeling." Before her performance, one notices that she feels מִתְרַגֶּשֶׁת (*mitrageshet*), nervous. Afterward, her heart is נִרְגָּשׁ (*nirgash*), touched, by the ovation she receives. A fan letter to the artist might be signed בְּרִגְשֵׁי כָּבוֹד (*be-rigshei kavod*), "Yours faithfully," literally, "with feelings of honor."

When a sentimentally bashful lover confesses יֵשׁ לִי רְגָשׁוֹת אֵלַיִךְ (*yesh li regashot elayikh*), I have feelings for you, what is your initial הַרְגָּשָׁה (*hargasha*), feeling?

When your driving instructor tells you that you are driving בְּלִי רֶגֶשׁ (*beli regesh*), he means that you lack a "feel" for it, because you are stepping too hard on the gas pedal. Depending on your personality, you may take his criticism בְּרְגָשׁוֹת מְעֹרָבִים (*birgashot me'oravim*), with mixed emotions. The practical thing, as 100 years of Hadassah have revealed, is to be מְרֻגָּשׁ (*merugash*), excited, to begin with.

91

Pursue Me If You Can

ר-ד-פ

resh-dalet-feh

How are Hebrew roots like the law? They both can be shaped to either nefarious or life-enhancing ends. Take the example of ר-ד-פ (*resh, dalet, feh*), to pursue or, in some cases, to chase away. The noun רוֹדֵף (*rodef*) means more than just pursuer. It is a term in Jewish jurisprudence for one who pursues another with the intent to kill. Jewish law states that a נִרְדָּף (*nirdaf*), one being pursued, has the right, even the responsibility, to slay a would-be slayer.

Tragically, Yigal Amir based his assassination of Israeli Prime Minister Yitzhak Rabin on the wrong-headed view that Rabin—in the eyes of the world a רוֹדֵף שָׁלוֹם (*rodef shalom*), pursuer of peace, in the tradition of the biblical Aaron—was a *rodef, tout court.* Jewish ethicists permit an abortion to save the life of a pregnant woman endangered by her pregnancy by declaring the fetus a *rodef.*

The root is found in Scripture most famously in the proclamation צֶדֶק צֶדֶק תִּרְדֹּף (*tsedek, tsedek tirdof*), "Justice, justice shalt thou pursue." It is also found in the 23rd Psalm in the verse, טוֹב וָחֶסֶד יִרְדְּפוּנִי (*tov va-hesed yirdefuni*), "May goodness and kindness pursue me." Psalm 34 enjoins, בַּקֵּשׁ שָׁלוֹם וְרָדְפֵהוּ (*bakesh shalom ve-rodfehu*), "Seek peace and run after it." A popular proverb in Jewish life teaches that הָרוֹדֵף אַחַר הַכָּבוֹד (*ha-rodef ahar ha-kavod*), "When one pursues honor, [honor flees]."

The Jerusalem Talmud describes a marriage custom that uses our root: רֶגֶל הַרְדוּפִין (*regel ha-redufin*), translated as the Festival of the Anxious. It seems that newlywed brides, anxious about their new condition, would try to return to their father's home to celebrate the first holiday falling after the wedding. The father would—gently, we hope—"chase" her back to her husband's home. Not to worry, the story implies. Just as יוֹם רוֹדֵף יוֹם (*yom rodef yom*), one day follows another in rapid succession, the bride will grow accustomed to her new surroundings.

A modern expression for a Casanova, translated not quite directly from the English, is רוֹדֵף שְׂמָלוֹת (*rodef semalot*), dress (i.e., skirt) chaser. Another sense of the root can be found in the form לְהִתְרַדֵּף (*le-hitradef*), to be dispersed—like a flock of sheep or like Jews in the diaspora.

How do we get the Hebrew expression for synonym, מִלָּה נִרְדֶּפֶת (*milla nirdefet*), literally, a pursued word? One might speculate that synonyms are so close together in meaning that it seems as though one word is being pursued by the other. There is also no harm in being a pursuer of words.

92

Higher and Higher

ר-ו-מ

resh-vav-mem

The primary goal at the Passover Seder is to recite in minutest detail stories surrounding the Exodus, right? Wrong. Often overlooked in the haggadah is a string of nine synonymous verbs telling us the importance of a further obligation: to praise God. One of these verbs, לְרוֹמֵם (*le-romem*), to exalt, has a lofty story to tell.

The root ר-ו-מ (*resh, vav, mem*), to rise high, is found throughout Scripture. Describing Noah's ark, the text recounts וַתָּרָם מֵעַל הָאָרֶץ (*va-taram me'al ha-aretz*), "It rose above the earth." How did Israel prevail in its battle with Amalek? It happened כַּאֲשֶׁר יָרִים מֹשֶׁה יָדוֹ (*ka'asher yarim moshe yado*), "when Moses held up his hand." The prophet Isaiah expresses God's disappointment in the children of Israel, asserting בָּנִים גִּדַּלְתִּי וְרוֹמַמְתִּי (*banim giddalti ve-romamti*), "I raised up children and they sinned against Me." One also finds the root in the names of such biblical personages as אַבְרָם (*avram*), Abram, before his name became Abraham; עַמְרָם (*amram*), Amram, father of Moses; and the prophet יִרְמְיָהוּ (*yirmiyahu*), Jeremiah—all three "exalted" figures.

In the first psalm recited in the haggadah, we are told the Lord is רָם עַל כָּל גּוֹיִם (*rom al kol goyim*), "above all nations." And in the liturgical section introduced by the *Nishmat* prayer, we recite בִּלְשׁוֹן חֲסִידִים תִּתְרוֹמָם (*bi-leshon hasidim titromam*), "God is to be praised in the mouths of the righteous."

The root's most lyrical use, perhaps, is found in "The Garden," a poem in praise of the Passover season by medieval Hebrew poet Moshe Ibn Ezra. He compares the flowering rose to a king כִּי עַל הוּרָם כִּסְאוֹ (*ki al huram kis'o*), "whose throne is raised on high." Speaking of kings, the root is found in the expression הוֹד

רוֹמְמוּתוֹ (*hod romemuto*), his highness, and likely in אַרְמוֹן (*armon*), palace, the tallest building in the kingdom.

The תְּרוּמָה (*teruma*), levy, was a priest's share of agricultural crops or dough for baking. Today, we can speak of a תְּרוּמַת אֵיבָרִים (*terumat evarim*), organ donation. A Hebrew University of Jerusalem fundraiser uses our root לְהָרִים תְּרוּמוֹת (*le-harim terumot*), to raise contributions, for its campus at גִּבְעַת רָם (*givat ram*), Givat Ram.

In America, Hebrew proficiency may be at a רָמָה נְמוּכָה (*rama nemukha*), low level, but Camp רָמָה (*rama*), Ramah, named for a biblical high place, is devoted to הֲרָמַת הָרָמָה (*haramat ha-rama*), raising the standards. A רַמְקוֹל (*ramkol*), loudspeaker, calls campers לְהָרִים דֶּגֶל (*le-harim degel*), to raise the flag.

On Passover eve, מְרִימִים קוֹלֵנוּ (*merimim kolenu*), we lift our voices, in song to the highest use of our root, לַמָּרוֹם (*la-marom*), toward heaven.

93

But Soft

ר-כ-כ

resh-khof-khof

R omeo, talking to himself in Juliet's courtyard, looks up and espies his beloved at her window. "But soft," he murmurs, meaning, let us praise her dazzling beauty in quiet tones. In the Oxford English Dictionary, the word "soft," aside from Shakespeare's sense of "quiet," can be found in as many as 50 different contexts. Similarly, the Hebrew ר-כ-כ (*resh, khof, khof*), to be soft, provides a plethora of meanings, including tender, mild, weak, delicate, timid, gentle and, even, cowardly.

In Genesis, that עֵינֵי לֵאָה רַכּוֹת (*einei lea rakkot*), "Leah's eyes were weak," is not an advantage. When, in Deuteronomy, the Israelites go to battle, the *kohen* heartens them with the watchword אַל יֵרַךְ לְבַבְכֶם (*al yerakh le-vavkhem*), literally "Let not your hearts soften," or do not let your courage falter. In a particularly bitter curse in Leviticus, God threatens וְהֵבֵאתִי מֹרֶךְ (*ve-heveiti morekh*), "I will cast the softness of cowardice into their hearts." Young King David in II Samuel, explaining his reluctance to seek vengeance for the murder of Abner, claims to be רַךְ וּמָשׁוּחַ מֶלֶךְ (*rakh u-meshu'ah melekh*), "a softy, even though anointed king." Oil is used in both anointments and ointments, and, as we read in Psalm 55, a certain ally cannot be trusted because רַכּוּ דְבָרָיו מִשֶּׁמֶן (*rakku devarav mi-shemen*), "his words [only] seem more soothing than oil."

The rabbis were especially fond of our root. In his commentaries on the Talmud, Rashi is both a romantic and a pragmatist. He notes sentimentally that the sound of weeping מְרַכֵּךְ לִבּוֹ שֶׁל אָדָם (*merakkekh libbo shel adam*), softens the heart of man; and, in a practical vein, that בְּגָדִים מִתְרַכְּכִין מִכִּבּוּסָם (*begadim mitrakekhin mi-kibbusam*), clothing gets soft in the laundering. While tractate Ta'anit proclaims that man should always be רַךְ כְּקָנֶה (*rakh kekaneh*), as flexible as a reed, the poet Solomon Ibn Gabirol asserts that a person שֶׁרַכּוּ פָּנָיו (*she-rakku panav*), who is too humble, becomes less wise.

Today, רְכִּיכוּת (*rekkikhut*), spinelessness, is used both clinically and metaphorically. A softening of the bones is a symptom of רַכֶּכֶת (*rakkekhet*), rickets. A בֵּיצָה רַכָּה (*beitsa rakka*), soft-boiled egg, makes for a healthy breakfast. We gaze tenderly at a רַךְ הַנּוֹלָד (*rakh ha-nolad*), newborn infant. Early childhood educators are trained to speak רַכּוֹת (*rakkot*), delicately, as they deal with children of גִּיל הָרַךְ (*gil ha-rakh*), tender preschool age.

If you are going to ask for a raise, it is wise לְרַכֵּךְ (*le-rakkekh*), to soften up, the boss first. And on your next flight—perhaps to pay a visit to Verona—may you have a נְחִיתָה רַכָּה (*nehita rakka*), a soft landing.

94

Let's NOT Talk About It

ר-כ-ל

resh-khof-lamed

Have you heard the one about the traveling salesman? No, not the one with the farmer's daughter: this one has to do with the Hebrew root ר-כ-ל (*resh, khof, lamed*) and its derivatives, רוֹכְלִים (*rokhlim*), biblical spice and perfume merchants, and הוֹלְכֵי רָכִיל (*holkhei rakhil*), rumormongers and scandalmongers. In the Jewish Publication Society's translation of the book of Proverbs, a *holekh rakhil* is described as a "base fellow, one who cannot keep a confidence to himself." Leviticus (19:16) has a more forbidding use for our root, commanding, לֹא תֵלֵךְ רָכִיל בְּעַמֶּיךָ (*lo telekh rakhil be-amekha*), "You shall not go up and down as a talebearer among your people."

Maimonides, in his *Mishneh Torah*, likens רְכִילוּת (*rekhilut*), gossip, to the shedding of blood. *Rekhilut* is often juxtaposed with שִׂמְחָה לְאֵיד (*simhah le-eid*), the pleasure taken in somebody else's misfortune, schadenfreude. *Rekhilut* is also used synonymously with לְשׁוֹן הָרַע (*leshon ha-ra*)—often pronounced *loshon horeh*—the evil tongue. Semantically speaking, and more to our point, *rekhilut* should be distinguished from רְכִילָה (*rekhilah*), the peddling of רְכֻלָּה (*rekhullah*), merchandise, at the מַרְכּוֹלֶת (*markolet*), market.

According to some linguists, however, the words רוֹכֵל (*rokhel*), itinerant peddler, and רְכֵל (*rekhel*), slanderous gossip, are related to, of all things, the word רֶגֶל (*regel*), foot. A hint: Are not the biblical מְרַגְּלִים (*meraglim*), a group of Israelites who spy out the Land of Israel and bring back a slanderous report, also מְרַכְּלִים (*merakhlim*), defamers? An even stronger proof is found in Psalms (15:3), which insists that only a person who has לֹא רָגַל עַל לְשׁוֹנוֹ (*lo regel al leshono*), "no slander upon his tongue," may dwell in the tent of the Lord.

In the Song of Songs, the expression אַבְקַת רוֹכֵל (*avkat rokhel*), literally, merchant's powder, refers to sweet-smelling spices and perfumes. The Talmud, in a lyrical mood, takes *avkat rokhel* metaphorically to refer to a great scholar.

In rabbinic Hebrew, the word רוֹכְלוֹת (*rokhlot*) denotes "success" on mercantile journeys. The prophet Ezekiel, however, uses our root four times to berate successful businessmen for their arrogance and self-importance. Reprimanding one who has grown haughty בְּרֹב חָכְמָתְךָ וּבְרְכֻלָּתְךָ (*be-rov hokhmatekha u-ve-rekhultekha*), "by your great shrewdness in trade," Ezekiel prophesies that one day "foreigners" will come to "strike down your splendor."

Today, life is more casual. When asked how last evening's gathering of friends went, one may be heard to reply, laconically, רְכַלְנוּ (*rikhalnu*), "We just shot the breeze." And for 30 years, that's what you and I have been doing.

95

Friends and Lovers

ר-ע-ה

resh-ayin-heh

In wedding season, one's thoughts turn naturally to...Hebrew. In terms of vocabulary, there is more to a Jewish wedding than חֲתוּנָה (*hatuna*), wedding; חוּפָּה (*huppa*), wedding canopy; קִדּוּשִׁין (*kiddushin*), sanctification of the union; and שֶׁבַע בְּרָכוֹת (*sheva berakhot*), seven blessings. There is also more than *machataynister*, that expressive feminine Yiddish word for mother-in-law—derived from the same root as *hatuna*. There is even more than חָתָן (*hatan*), groom, and כַּלָּה (*kalla*), bride.

There are רֵעִים אֲהוּבִים (*re'im ahuvim*), loving companions, as seen in the wedding liturgy's שַׂמֵּחַ תְּשַׂמַּח רֵעִים הָאֲהוּבִים (*same'ah tisamah re'im ha-ahuvim*), "Rejoice over the loving companions." The wedding ceremony emphasizes further that a good relationship requires love, fraternity, peace and רֵעוּת (*re'ut*), friendship. Because Ruth is the paradigm of the רַעְיָה (*ra'aya*), wife, some scholars contend that her name in the book of Ruth comes from *re'ut*.

The root ר-ע-ה (*resh, ayin, heh*), to associate with, contains the essence of many a successful relationship. According to Rabbi Akiva, the most important commandment in the Torah is: וְאָהַבְתָּ לְרֵעֲךָ כָּמוֹךָ (*ve-ahavta le-re'akha ka-mokha*), "You shall love your neighbor as yourself." In the Song of Songs, the beloved is called many romantic things, the most poignant of which is רַעְיָתִי (*ra'yati*), my companion. The root appears in the last two of the Ten Commandments, ordaining that you not bear false witness against nor covet the wife or house of רֵעֶךָ (*re'ekha*), your neighbor. The book of Proverbs warns אַל תִּתְרַע אֶת בַּעַל אָף (*al titra et ba'al af*), "Don't become the companion of a bad-tempered man."

The Talmud uses the expression יַגִּיד עָלָיו רֵעוֹ (*yaggid alav re'o*), literally, let its neighbor tell us of it, when it needs to learn the particulars of one law from a similar law. The technical term for a word that appears only once in the *Tanakh* is the Greek expression *hapax legomenon*. In Hebrew, one says אֵין לוֹ רֵעַ בַּמִּקְרָא (*ein lo re'a ba-mikra*), it has no companion in Scripture. Of a unique event in history, one says *ein lo re'a*, it has no equal. The root often appears in tandem with the word for brother, as in לְמַעַן אַחַי וְרֵעָי (*le-ma'an ahai ve-re'ai*), for the sake of my brothers and companions.

Then there is the expression רֵעִי כְּאָח לִי (*re'i ke-ah li*), my companion is like a brother to me. In marriage, perhaps that is taking a good thing like friendship too far. That is precisely where אַהֲבָה (*ahava*), love, should reassert its place.

96

Where There's a Will There's a Story

ר-צ-ה
resh-tsadi-heh

In Israel, even birds have free will. Humorist Dan Ben Amotz relates that, at a time when Israeli coffee was truly undrinkable, a man tried to smuggle in—as bird food—a whole suitcase of European coffee. Ingenuously, the customs official asks, "Do you mean to tell me that birds eat coffee?" Without blinking an eye, our crafty Israeli responds, יִרְצוּ יֹאכְלוּ; לֹא יִרְצוּ, לֹא יֹאכְלוּ (*yirtsu yokhlu; lo yirtsu, lo yokhlu*), "If they want, they'll eat; if they don't, they won't." Obviously, people felt they could use the root ר-צ-ה (*resh, tsadi, heh*), to want, however they wanted. Indeed, the root has several other meanings, including to satisfy (a person or a debt), accept, love and even lecture.

In Scripture, victorious Mordecai is רָצוּי (*ratsui*), beloved, of his brethren. One of the daughters of Zelophehad, whose petition for equal inheritance rights is accepted by God, is called תִּרְצָה (*tirtsa*), "pleasing." The psalmist praises God's beneficence, "You open your hand and" מַשְׂבִּיעַ לְכָל חַי רָצוֹן (*masbi'a le-khol hai ratson*), "satisfy the desires of every living thing."

Sometimes, God satisfies too much. In a charming talmudic story, miracle worker Honi the Circle Maker prays for rain and gets a flood. He admonishes God that he wanted גִּשְׁמֵי רָצוֹן (*gishmei ratson*), "enough rain," but not an inundation. In a deft rabbinic move, though one may not compel a divorce, one may use force on a recalcitrant husband until he says רוֹצֶה אֲנִי (*rotseh ani*), I'm eager. The root is also found abundantly in Jewish ritual practice. Probably the most frequently enunciated Jewish expression is אִם יִרְצֶה הַשֵּׁם (*im yirtseh ha-shem*), God willing. The most propitious time for soliciting God's favor is עֵת רָצוֹן (*et ratson*), when God is especially disposed to respond to prayers. In the *Amidah* prayer, we entreat

God, רְצֵה (*retseh*), may you be pleased with your people Israel. Toward the end of the Passover haggadah, we proclaim נִרְצָה (*nirtsah*), the Seder has been performed in a manner acceptable to God.

A מַרְצֶה (*martseh*), lecturer, may ask, are you מְרוּצֶה (*merutseh*), satisfied, with your studies? In statecraft it is never good strategy לְרַצּוֹת (*le-ratsot*), to appease, an enemy. Nevertheless, a diplomat must balance הָרָצוּי וְהַמָּצוּי (*ha-ratsui ve-ha-matsui*), the desirable and the available. A Hebrew-speaking romantic hero will need only one word to address his princess bride, כִּרְצוֹנֵךְ (*kirtsonekh*), "As you wish." And let us not forget the Hebrew version of Theodor Herzl's *Altneuland*, which promises אִם תִּרְצוּ, אֵין זוֹ אַגָּדָה (*im tirtsu, ein zo aggadah*), "If you will it, it is no fairytale." A State called Israel coming into being is, nevertheless, a good story.

97

The Numbers Game

שׁ-ב-ע
shin-vet-ayin

Ever since God gave the Third Commandment—against taking His name in vain—oaths have been frowned upon in Judaism. This raises not only theological and sociological questions, but perhaps a linguistic one, too. To get to the word שְׁבוּעָה (*shevu'a*), oath, we have to play a numbers game and look first at שֶׁבַע (*sheva*), seven, which shares the same root: שׁ-ב-ע (*shin, vet, ayin*). Are the two connected? And, if so, how?

The number seven is found throughout Jewish life: there are the שֶׁבַע בְּרָכוֹת (*sheva berakhot*), seven blessings, said at a wedding; the holiday of שָׁבוּעוֹת (*shavu'ot*), Pentecost, which comes seven weeks after Passover; the שִׁבְעָה (*shiva*), seven-day mourning period; and the greeting שָׁבוּעַ טוֹב (*shavu'a tov*), good week. In Israel, there is also the liberating סוֹף שָׁבוּעַ (*sof shavu'a*), weekend, and the שְׁבִיעִיָּה (*shvi'iyya*), septet, at the concert hall.

As in other ancient cultures, the number seven is revered in Judaism, denoting large quantity. In Scripture, the root is found first in Genesis, when God reassures Cain that if he is killed, his death will be avenged שִׁבְעָתַיִם (*shivatayim*), "sevenfold"—a hyperbolic phrase that could mean any vaguely large amount. The Hebrew name for Elizabeth, אֱלִישֶׁבַע (*elisheva*), literally, my God is sevenfold, may be an early iteration of the expression "God is great."

In Hebrew, the root can be turned into a passive verb—which brings us to an oath. God reminds his people constantly of the land אֲשֶׁר נִשְׁבַּעְתִּי (*asher nishbati*), "that I promised," to Abraham. Although it sounds far-fetched, the expression means something like "the land that I bound myself seven times to give to Abraham." In a related example, Abraham resolves a waterhole dispute by agreeing to swear an oath: אָנֹכִי אִשָּׁבֵעַ (*anokhi ishave'a*), "I will be bound seven times," that is, I will swear. And that brings us straight to the city of

בְּאֵר שֶׁבַע (*be'er sheva*), Beersheba. As the Torah explains, the בְּאֵר (*be'er*), well, was called Beersheba because שָׁם נִשְׁבְּעוּ שְׁנֵיהֶם (*sham nishbe'u shenei-hem*), "there the two of them [Abraham and Abimelekh] took an oath."

One commentator speculates that, alternatively, Sheva could have been the name of the owner of the well in question. Does not II Samuel introduce a certain שֶׁבַע בֶּן בִּכְרִי (*sheva ben bikhri*), Sheva Ben Bikhri, who revolted against King David? If you are not satisfied with this, then just turn the page. That's where we will move the dot from the right side of the שׁ (*shin*) to the left side, turning it into the letter שׂ (*sin*), and talk about another root, שׂ-ב-ע (*sin, vet, ayin*), to be satisfied. We promise. Seven times. Satisfaction Guaranteed.

98

Satisfaction Guaranteed

שׁ-ב-ע

sin-vet-ayin

There are some people who, especially in times of distress, financial or otherwise, can't get any satisfaction. The Hebrew root שׁ-ב-ע (*sin, vet, ayin*), to be satisfied, sated, takes us back to a time when satisfaction with one's lot was a norm. When Abraham died, he was זָקֵן וְשָׂבֵעַ (*zaken ve-save'a*), "old and contented." Even Isaac, who had been traumatized by being bound on an altar, and Job, the epitome of suffering who had complained that humankind is שְׂבַע רֹגֶז (*seva rogez*), "sated with trouble," each died זָקֵן וּשְׂבַע יָמִים (*zaken u-seva yamim*), "in ripe old age." Moses, blessing the tribes of Israel at the end of his life, singles out Naftali as שְׂבַע רָצוֹן (*seva ratson*), "sated with God's favor."

The book of Ecclesiastes comes to our root via a homily on human nature, asserting אֹהֵב כֶּסֶף לֹא יִשְׂבַּע כֶּסֶף (*ohev kesef lo yisba kesef*), "A lover of money never has his fill of money." In a similar vein, a popular proverb declares אֵין הַקּוֹמֶץ מַשְׂבִּיעַ אֶת הָאֲרִי (*ein ha-komets masbi'a et ha-ari*), a mere handful does not satisfy the lion. The Prayers for Dew and Rain conclude with the exclamation לְשׂוֹבַע וְלֹא לְרָזוֹן (*le-sova ve-lo le-razon*), [may this moisture be] for plenty and not for scarcity!

Originally, the root had to do with food and with the feeling of being שָׂבֵעַ (*save'a*), full, and therefore no longer hungry. Deuteronomy states וְאָכַלְתָּ וְשָׂבָעְתָּ וּבֵרַכְתָּ (*ve-ak halta ve-savata u-verakhta*), "after you have eaten your fill, you should say a blessing." (A restaurant menu may add: *ve-shilamta*, and you should pay your bill.) The rabbis taught, based on this verse, that to say Grace After Meals requires שְׂבִיעָה (*sevi'a*), being satiated—for them an egg would do. The Passover lamb must also be eaten בְּשׂבַע (*be-sova*), to one's satiety. Maimonides, in his *Guide to the Perplexed*, praises the person who is שְׂבַע נֶפֶשׁ (*seva nefesh*), satisfied in his soul, and therefore satisfied with little.

The most charming story having to do with our root is found in a midrash on I Samuel. The handsome young Saul meets a group of girls on his way to visit the Prophet Samuel, prior to being anointed king. He asks them if Samuel is at home. Instead of a simple "yes," they stretch out their reply into several long sentences. The midrash interprets the maidens' drawn out response as a tactic to delay Saul's leave-taking, concluding, לֹא שָׂבְעוּ לִרְאוֹת (*lo sav'u lirot*), they just couldn't get enough of looking at Saul's beauty.

That is quite possibly the last time this tragic king was, as we use the term today, שְׂבַע רָצוֹן (*seva ratson*), happy with his lot.

99

The Seventh Day

שׁ-ב-ת

shin-vet-tav

There are those who hear the Akkadian word for festival, *shappatu*, as a possible ancestor of the Hebrew word Shabbat. But, insists etymologist Ernest Klein, the concept of a weekly day of rest is the gift of the Hebrew language to the world. The root שׁ-ב-ת (*shin, vet, tav*), to cease from labor, has many uses today, in both religious and secular contexts. One might even say that in the 55 years since the Six-Day War, the Zionist world has not taken a שַׁבָּת (*shabbat*), "day off," from debating that war's consequences.

Shabbat is linguistically wide-ranging, a feminine singular noun that is sometimes masculine and, in the *Amidah* of the Shabbat afternoon service, plural as well. Lexically varied, Shabbat is not only the seventh *day* of the week. It is also a *week*, one of שֶׁבַע שַׁבָּתוֹת (*sheva shabbatot*), seven Sabbaths, between Passover and Shavuot. The expression שַׁבָּת שַׁבָּתוֹן (*shabbat shabbaton*), refers not only to Yom Kippur but also to the sabbatical year, when the land lies fallow (and academics on *shabbaton* do research). Shabbat is also eternity, i.e., the world to come, יוֹם שֶׁכֻּלּוֹ שַׁבָּת (*yom she-kulo shabbat*), the "day that is all Shabbat." In the expression מִמָּחֳרַת הַשַּׁבָּת (*mi-mohorat ha-shabbat*), "from the day after Shabbat," when we begin to count the *omer*, the word Shabbat refers to the first day of Passover. The phrase וַיִּשְׁבֹּת בַּיּוֹם הַשְּׁבִיעִי (*va-yishbot ba-yom ha-shevi'i*), "He/It ceased on the seventh day," is applied to both the God of Creation and the manna falling from heaven. When workers today wish to protest, they go on שְׁבִיתָה (*shevitah*), strike.

Rabbi Akiva reportedly offered the following advice to his son: rather than rely on others, if you can't afford a meal that is שַׁבָּתִי (*shabbati*), festive, עֲשֵׂה שַׁבָּתְךָ חֹל (*aseh shabbatekha hol*), "Make your Sabbath a weekday." The Jerusalem Talmud tells a quaint story about the legendary river סַמְבַּטְיוֹן (*sambatyon*). The river takes a day off from its hazardous weekday rock-heaving turbulence on Shabbat, the day, ironically, when Jews may not cross rivers. One of the most beautiful modern Shabbat hymns, Hayim Nahman Bialik's שַׁבָּת הַמַּלְכָּה (*shabbat ha-malkah*), "The Sabbath Queen," rewrites a story told in the Talmud of a pair of ministering angels who visit on לֵיל שַׁבָּת (*leil shabbat*), Friday evening.

    Shabbat is when עִבְרִית שֶׁל שַׁבָּת (*ivrit shel shabbat*), dignified Hebrew, and עוֹנֶג שַׁבָּת (*oneg shabbat*), decorous pleasure, rule the day. No matter our political differences after more than 50 years, the time is always right for the greeting שַׁבָּת שָׁלוֹם (*shabbat shalom*).

100

Jews: The Musical

שׁ-י-ר

shin-yod-resh

From Moses to Miriam, from Deborah to David, when our Israelite leaders had something important to say, they frequently said it in song. The Hebrew root שׁ-י-ר (*shin, yod, resh*), to sing, is an organic part of the Jewish character. Indeed, despite appearances to the contrary, Jewish history itself may be seen as one immense musical—in both a major and a minor key.

The best-known use of our root in Scripture is שִׁיר הַשִּׁירִים (*shir ha-shirim*), the Song of Songs, the love poem attributed to King Solomon. Close behind is the Song at the Sea, beginning אָז יָשִׁיר (*az yashir*), "Then Moses sang," after the parting of the Sea of Reeds. This gave rise to an ethical admonishment proclaimed by God, recorded in the Talmud: "My creatures are drowning in the sea, וְאַתֶּם אוֹמְרִים שִׁירָה (*ve-atem omerim shira*), and you sing poetry?"

Among the treasures amassed by King Solomon are שָׁרִים וְשָׁרוֹת (*sharim ve-sharot*), male and female singers. There is also, in Isaiah, שִׁירַת הַזּוֹנָה (*shirat ha-zona*), the harlot's ditty—but we won't get into that. Better to focus on שִׁיר הַמַּעֲלוֹת (*shir ha-ma'alot*), the Song of Ascents, so called, according to some scholars, because the 15 psalms were sung by the Levites on the staircase leading to the Temple.

One of the greatest periods of Jewish cultural history is represented by שִׁירַת סְפָרַד (*shirat sefarad*), the poetry of Spain. The call of בַּת הַשִּׁיר (*bat ha-shir*), the poetic muse, during that era is found in a poem by Moses Ibn Ezra: מֵיטַב הַשִּׁיר כְּזָבוֹ (*metav ha-shir kezavo*), "the essence of a poem is its deceitfulness," emphasizing the poem's purported metaphorical truths.

There is probably no era in Israel more devoted to song than the present one. Step into almost any community center and you will be treated to an evening of שִׁירָה בְּצִבּוּר (*shira be-tzibbur*), communal singing. Despite the fact that Israelis like to make fun of their patriotic songs—calling them mockingly שִׁירֵי סוֹכְנוּת (*shirei sokhnut*), songs of the Jewish Agency—nevertheless they are not embarrassed to belt them out when gathered among friends. Light music is called שִׁירֵי גַּלְגַּלָץ (*shirei galgalatz*), deriving its name from the Army radio station, *Galei Tzahal*.

Because everybody has at least one more song left, few people are willing to acknowledge that they are singing their שִׁירַת הַבַּרְבּוּר (*shirat ha-barbur*), swan song. As מְשׁוֹרֵר (*meshorer*), poet, Natan Alterman says of the Israeli pioneers in the Jewish Agency's שִׁירוֹן (*shiron*), songbook, הַשִּׁיר לֹא תָּם (*ha-shir lo tam*), the song has not ended. It's just beginning.

101

Making Sense of It All

שׂ-כ-ל

sin-khof-lamed

Maimonides, the great Jewish philosopher, suggests that there are two types of people: those who order their lives through feelings and those who approach life using their שֵׂכֶל (*sekhel*), intellect. There are also two types of Jewish precepts: מִצְווֹת שִׁמְעִיּוֹת (*mitsvot shim'iyyot*), precepts one obeys because one has "heard" of them through the tradition, and מִצְווֹת שִׂכְלִיּוֹת (*mitsvot sikhliyyot*), precepts one has arrived at through the use of reason. These deep thoughts take us to the root שׂ-כ-ל (*sin, khof, lamed*), wisdom, success, cunning, good eyesight, good looks and a mystical power to change the natural order of things.

In Scripture, King Saul becomes jealous of the praise heaped on young David, who יַשְׂכִּיל (*yaskil*), succeeded, in all his military exploits. When the Psalmist proclaims מִכָּל מְלַמְּדַי הִשְׂכַּלְתִּי (*mi-kol melamdai hiskalti*), is he modestly implying, "I have learned from all my teachers [even from those less well educated than myself]"? Or is he boasting, "I have exceeded all my teachers in wisdom"?

In the story of the Garden of Eden, the Tree of Knowledge is described as נֶחְמָד...לְהַשְׂכִּיל (*nehmad...le-haskil*), "desirable as a source of wisdom." At the same time, *le-haskil* also means "to observe," making the tree also "a delight to look at."

Similarly, Abigail, who resolves to her own benefit the conflict between her boorish husband, Nabal, and the dashing future King David, is טוֹבַת שֵׂכֶל (*tovat sekhel*), a woman of great cunning—and good to look at.

When Joseph's sons are brought to Jacob for a blessing, the wily old man שִׂכֵּל אֶת יָדָיו (*sikkel et yadav*), crossed his hands, so that the right hand lay on the younger son. According to Rashi, based on the Aramaic translation of the word *sikkel*, the hands themselves were mystically empowered with the wisdom to modify the laws of primogeniture.

The title מַשְׂכִּיל (*maskil*)—today, any enlightened person—was given to the disciples of Moses Mendelssohn (1729–1786), the progenitor of the הַשְׂכָּלָה (*haskalah*), the Jewish Enlightenment, with הַשְׂכָּלָה גְּבוֹהָה (*haskalah gevohah*) today being higher education.

In Israel, one finds our root translated from English, variously, as John Locke's מַסָּה עַל שֵׂכֶל הָאָדָם (*massah al sekhel ha-adam*), *An Essay Concerning Human Understanding*; Roger Hargreaves' children's book, גְּבֶרֶת שֵׂכֶל (*geveret sekhel*, *Little Miss Brainy*; and the rock group כְּנֵסִיַּית הַשֵּׂכֶל (*kenessiat ha-sekhel*), The Church of Reason.

The root is even found on the home page of the Hebrew version of Google, where the expression "I'm feeling lucky" is rendered as יוֹתֵר מַזָּל מִשֵּׂכֶל (*yoter mazzal mi-sekhel*), "More Luck Than Brains." You can Google it yourself.

102

Guardian Angels

שׁ-מ-ר

shin-mem-resh

What connects Purim, Passover and the New York Police Department? Each uses the Hebrew root שׁ-מ-ר (*shin, mem, resh*), to guard, keep, preserve. On Purim, we read the book of Esther, which refers to שֹׁמֵר הַנָּשִׁים (*shomer ha-nashim*), the women's attendant. For Passover, one guards *matzot* and many people eat מַצָּה שְׁמוּרָה (*matsa shemura*), made with harvested wheat "guarded" from dampness and therefore from fermentation. And the police? Think of the Shomrim Society, NYPD's fraternal organization of Jewish "guardians."

Much of the Bible's use of the root has made its way into everyday parlance, such as Cain's הֲשֹׁמֵר אָחִי אָנֹכִי? (*ha-shomer ahi anokhi*), "Am I my brother's keeper?" Deuteronomy's version of the Fourth Commandment, שָׁמוֹר אֶת יוֹם הַשַּׁבָּת (*shamor et yom ha-shabbat*), observe, or celebrate, the Sabbath, gives us שׁוֹמֵר שַׁבָּת (*shomer shabbat*), Sabbath observer.

How do we know we're supposed to take care of ourselves? From a creative reading of Deuteronomy's וְנִשְׁמַרְתֶּם...לְנַפְשֹׁתֵיכֶם (*ve-nishmartem le-nafshotei-khem*), "Be...careful what you do." And that we're supposed to pay pledges to charity? From מוֹצָא שְׂפָתֶיךָ תִּשְׁמֹר (*motsa sefatekha tishmor*), "Keep to what comes out of your lips." And that we're supposed to be careful when we write checks? That comes from a previous generation's pun on Scripture. They took a biblical expression, הִשָּׁמֶר לְךָ פֶּן (*hishamer lekha pen*), "Be careful lest you..." and read the last word as English, as in watch what you do with your pen.

Speaking of playfulness, 17th-century Venetian rabbi Leone Modena wrote a Hebrew poem beginning קִינָה שְׁמוֹר (*kina shemor*), "Pay heed to this elegy"; all of its verses can also be pronounced in Italian, commencing with *Chi nasce muor*, "Whoever is born dies."

Two English words heard frequently in modern Hebrew are תֶּרְמוֹס (*termos*), thermos, and בֵּייבִּיסִיטֶר (*beibisiter*), babysitter. They have Hebrew equivalents deriving from our root—שְׁמוֹרחֹם (*shemorhom*), keeps the heat, and שְׁמַרטַף (*shemartaf*), watches the infant.

While it is not always good to be שַׁמְרָנִי (*shamrani*), conservative, it is always a pleasure to visit an Israeli שְׁמוּרַת טֶבַע (*shemurat teva*), nature preserve. A small but important bodily guardian is the שְׁמוּרָה (*shemura*), eyelid. Those of us on the substantial side might want to participate in a group of שׁוֹמְרֵי מִשְׁקָל (*shomrei mishkal*), weight watchers. Civic-minded Israelis will often volunteer for מִשְׁמָר אֶזְרָחִי (*mishmar ezrahi*), civil defense.

If you want to quote from this column, go ahead. But don't forget, כָּל הַזְּכוּיוֹת שְׁמוּרוֹת (*kol ha-zekhuyot shemurot*), all rights are reserved.

103

Judgment Calls

שׁ-פ-ט

shin-feh-tet

Soon after the nomination of Judge Michael Mukasey for United States attorney general, the Jewish media began buzzing that, despite his Irish-sounding name, he is a practicing Jew. Scooping them all, we have a further revelation: the שׁוֹפֵט (*shofet*), judge, is also a Hebrew-speaker. Indeed, his Hebrew comes from Camp Massad's playing fields—where a *shofet* was a baseball umpire. Leaning heavily on legalism, Jewish culture permits especially wide latitude in the case of the root שׁ-פ-ט (*shin, feh, tet*), to judge.

In Scripture, Abraham takes God to task for his willingness to destroy the righteous of Sodom, asking הֲשֹׁפֵט כָּל הָאָרֶץ לֹא יַעֲשֶׂה מִשְׁפָּט (*ha-shofet kol ha-arets lo ya'aseh mishpat*), "Shall not the Judge of all the earth deal justly?" Aaron's חֹשֶׁן מִשְׁפָּט (*hoshen mishpat*), pouch of decision, was worn by the high priest as an oracular breastplate. The tribute paid to priests is called מִשְׁפַּט הַכֹּהֲנִים (*mishpat ha-kohanim*), the priests' due. The root's meaning broadens when, to explain away King David's ruthless treatment of his enemies, we are told simply, כֹּה מִשְׁפָּטוֹ (*ko mishpato*), "that was his habitual practice." The traditional translation of the title of סֵפֶר שׁוֹפְטִים (*sefer shoftim*), the book of Judges, is misleading: we realize this when the Israelites ask Samuel for a king לְשָׁפְטֵנוּ (*le-shoftenu*), "to govern us." And then there is the book of Ruth, set in a period when שְׁפֹט הַשֹּׁפְטִים (*shefot ha-shoftim*), "the chieftains ruled."

The midrash takes this expression literally for homiletical purposes, saying, woe to the generation שֶׁשֹּׁפְטָיו צְרִיכִין לְהִשָּׁפֵט (*she-shoftav tserikhin le-hishafet*), whose judges themselves should be judged. Similarly, the rabbis took from Jeremiah the phrase לַבֹּקֶר מִשְׁפָּט (*la-boker mishpat*), "judgment in the morning," to admonish us not to judge too quickly. In the Passover haggadah, the phrase

וְעָשָׂה בָהֶם שְׁפָטִים (*ve-asa va-hem shefatim*) provides another meaning of our root—to punish.

Kobi Oz, the lead singer of the Israeli band Teapacks, tells us that when his girlfriend starts to bawl, אֲנִי שָׁפוּט שֶׁלָּה (*ani shafut shella*), "I am her prisoner [of love]." Today, you can speak not only of מִשְׁפְּטָנוּת (*mishpetanut*), jurisprudence, but also of grammar: a מִשְׁפָּט (*mishpat*) is a sentence in both law and language. In some courts, you will find a שׁוֹפֵט (*shofet*), jurist, and a שׁוֹפֵט מֻשְׁבָּע (*shofet mushba*), juror. Appeals lawyers and tour guides both recommend their clients visit בֵּית הַמִּשְׁפָּט הָעֶלְיוֹן (*beit ha-mishpat ha-elyon*), Israel's Supreme Court. Like a good attorney general, one should go without מִשְׁפָּט קָדוּם (*mishpat kadum*), prejudice.

104

It's Time to Upgrade

שׁ-פ-ר

shin-feh-resh

Why do we blow a שׁוֹפָר (*shofar*) and not a קֶרֶן (*keren*), horn, on Rosh Hashanah? After all, in the Akedah story, which we commemorate with the blowing of the *shofar*, the ram was caught in the brambles not by its *shofar* but בְּקַרְנָיו (*be-karnav*), by its horns. The answer, like a *shofar*, has many twists and turns. It all comes down to the root שׁ-פ-ר (*shin, feh, resh*), to be pleasing, handsome, to improve, beautify.

No one knows exactly what the expression אִמְרֵי שָׁפֶר (*imrei shefer*) in Genesis 49:21 refers to. One etymologist suggests that *shefer* means antlers, "in allusion to their beauty." For others, *imrei shefer* means, variously, lovely fawns, lovely treetops or beautifully constructed speeches.

Samson Raphael Hirsch, for whom *shefer* connotes a beauty that is "arched, curved, harmonious," relates the word to both שַׁפְרוּר (*shafrur*), circular pavilion, and *shofar*, the sinuous ram's horn. For others, *shofar*, like שְׁפוֹפֶרֶת (*shefoferet*), telephone receiver, is a curved instrument that conducts sounds. Some say the term שָׁפִיר (*shapir*), placenta, because of its curvature, is related to these words.

There is also a rabbinical expression, אִמְרֵי שׁוֹפָר (*imrei shofar*), taken homiletically to mean that the sounds of the *shofar* harmonize the words of the Torah. The *shofar* also musically calls out to us: שַׁפְּרוּ מַעֲשֵׂיכֶם (*shapru ma'a-seikhem*), improve your deeds.

At the fruit market, the greengrocer will assure you that his melons are, Aramaically speaking, שׁוּפְרָא דְּשׁוּפְרָא (*shufra de-shufra*), the best of the best. In the Sabbath hymn "*Yah Ribbon*" we use the root twice: singing שְׁפַר קֳדָמָךְ לְהַחֲוַיָּא (*shefar kadamakh le-hahavayya*), "It is pleasant to declare [your wondrous deeds] before you"; and proclaiming that Jerusalem is קַרְתָּא דְּשׁוּפְרַיָּא (*karta de-shufrayya*), "the city of beauty."

In the old days, an אַשְׁפָּר (*ashpar*) was a tailor who mended old clothes; today, we call that person a חַיָּט (*hayyat*) and use *ashpar* (or, more commonly, שַׁפָּר (*shapar*), for someone who does makeovers, a home decorator: the word אַשְׁפָּרָה (*ashpara*) is used for the chemical process of finishing textiles.

When French-Jewish crooner Enrico Macias appeared in concert in Jerusalem, he dazzled the crowd not only with his French songs, but also with his spoken Hebrew. To the crowd's applause, he crowed, "הָעִבְרִית שֶׁלִּי מִשְׁתַּפֶּרֶת, לֹא?" (*ha-ivrit sheli mishtaperet, lo?*), "My Hebrew's getting better, isn't it?" Was Macias tooting his own *shofar*? At least he was setting a good example for us all.

105

It's Purim; Let's Party

שׁ-ת-ה

shin-tav-heh

Purim is a topsy-turvy holiday. By encouraging us to invert the norms of communal behavior, Purim teaches us the boundaries of those norms.

Take the example of שְׁתִיָּה (*shetiyyah*), drinking. The rabbis tell us that on Purim, contrary to normative Jewish behavior, we are supposed to get so שָׁתוּי (*shatui*), drunk, that we bless evil Haman and curse heroic Mordecai. This example of rabbinic thinking is more nuanced in the Purim story itself, recounted in the book of Esther. There, the Hebrew root שׁ-ת-ה (*shin, tav, heh*), to drink, plays a starring role.

This is so in the word מִשְׁתֶּה (*mishteh*), drinking party or banquet. The book of Esther begins with a gala *mishteh* given by the king, followed by a מִשְׁתֵּה נָשִׁים (*mishteh nashim*), "women's party" offered by the queen. Some grammarians suggest that the lack of a preposition between these two Hebrew nouns means that the party was particularly "womanly" in style and content. When Esther later accedes to Vashti's throne, she hosts not one *mishteh* but two מִשְׁתָּאוֹת (*mishta'ot*) or מִשְׁתִּים (*mishtim*), parties—neither of these masculine plural words is found in Scripture—dramatizing her goal of unmasking Haman's evil plot against the Jews.

Among other *mishteh* hosts in the Torah are Abraham, on the day Isaac is weaned; and Laban, to celebrate the marriage he engineers between his elder daughter, Leah, and Jacob. Today's custom of celebrating a marriage with *sheva brakhot*, seven parties, literally, seven blessings, is attributed to Samson's שִׁבְעַת יְמֵי הַמִּשְׁתֶּה (*shiv'at yemei ha-mishteh*), seven feast days, rejoicing at his ill-fated marriage to a Philistine woman. Maybe that's why Ecclesiastes declares that it is better to frequent a house of mourning than a בֵּית מִשְׁתֶּה (*beit mishteh*), house of feasting.

The root for לִשְׁתּוֹת (*lishtot*), to drink, appears more than 200 times in Scripture, most movingly in the story of Abraham's servant, sent to secure a wife for his master's son. The servant recognizes that Rebecca is appropriate when, at a well, she says to him, שְׁתֵה (*sheteh*), drink, "and I will also draw water for your camels." The rabbis of *Pirke Avot* use the root metaphorically when they advise לִשְׁתּוֹת בְּצָמָא דִּבְרֵיהֶם (*lishtot be-tsama divreihem*), "to drink the words of the Sages thirstily."

Today, at the office, one proffers a שְׁתִיָּה (*shetiyyah*), toast, a modest drinking ceremony to celebrate a successful team job. When a task is handled foolishly the boss may ask מַה שָּׁתִיתָ (*mah shatitah*), what have you been drinking? On Purim, of course, it's always the opposite.

106

Partners & Co.

שׁ-ת-פּ

shin-tav-feh

The word socialism has been bandied about a lot lately in American political discourse, almost always with a vituperative, accusatory tone. This was, of course, not the case at the founding of the modern State of Israel, when socialism flourished. Nevertheless, neither שַׁתְּפָנוּת (*shatfanut*), socialism, nor שַׁתְּפָן (*shatfan*), socialist, is a traditional Jewish concept. How do we know? It is a matter of vocabulary. The Hebrew root שׁ-ת-פּ (*shin, tav, feh*), to join, combine, attach, from which *shatfanut* derives, is nowhere to be found in the Hebrew Bible.

Absent from the *Tanakh*, the Aramaic form of the root is certainly prevalent in rabbinic literature. The midrash on Genesis suggests that, for Jacob, all his sons except Benjamin were שֻׁתָּפִין (*shutafin*), complicit, in the sale of Joseph. The Talmud warns that when a pot belongs to two שֻׁתָּפֵי (*shutafei*), partners, the pot may not be "hot or cold," i.e., advantageous to either. Samuel Ibn Tibbon, Maimonides's translator, uses the expression שֵׁם מְשֻׁתָּף (*shem me-shutaf*), shared noun, to describe homonyms that have several meanings. An old rabbinic saying has it that שֻׁתָּף לְסְטִים (*shutaf listim*), a robber's accomplice, is no better than a robber.

If you cannot remember seeing the word שׁוּתָּף (*shutaf*), partner, lately, go for a walk on any commercial street in Israel where you are likely to find signs with an abbreviation derived from our root, on the model of כֹּהֵן וְשׁוּת' (*kohen ve-shut[afav]*), Cohen and Co. If that doesn't work, think back to your childhood, when your Yiddish-speaking uncle would talk about his *shittif*, partner. Today, many Israeli apartment dwellers live in a בַּיִת מְשֻׁתָּף (*bayit meshutaf*), co-op. According to language maven Ruvik Rosenthal, the Hebrew abbreviation מַשְׁתַּפ (*mashtap*), from the expression מְשַׁתֵּף פְּעוּלָה (*meshatef pe'ulah*), one who cooperates, is used by the Shin Bet security service to describe a counterspy. In another setting, a courtesy you are asked for is likely to conclude with תּוֹדָה עַל שִׁיתּוּף הַפְּעוּלָה (*todah al shittuf ha-pe'ulah*), "Thank you for your cooperation." The mathematical מְכַנֶּה מְשֻׁתָּף (*mekhaneh meshutaf*), common denominator, is also used to express commonality between two people.

Have you ever received an invitation in Hebrew for a fundraising event? It is most likely being held with the הִשְׁתַּתְּפוּת (*hishtatfut*), participation, of a celebrity. When you have good news, you will want לְשַׁתֵּף (*le-shatef*), to share, your announcement with a close friend. That person will certainly מְשַׁתֵּף בְּשִׂמְחָתְךָ (*mishtatef be-simhatkha*), share in your happiness—by sharing the wealth perhaps—with or without socialist intentions.

107

Insider Traiting

ת-ו-כ

tav-vav-khof

What are the traits that distinguish an insider from an outsider? For one thing, an outsider may know what's happening; an insider understands what's going on. The Hebrew insider goes deep inside a root to bring out its hidden treasures. Take the example of ת-ו-כ (*tav, vav, khof*), originally, to pierce or halve; subsequently it has been used mainly as a noun, meaning the inside or the center.

The root is found prominently in Scripture to emphasize centrality. On the second day of creation God forms a firmament בְּתוֹךְ הַמָּיִם (*be-tokh ha-mayim*), "in the midst of the waters." Designing Eden, God puts the Tree of Life בְּתוֹךְ הַגָּן (*be-tokh ha-gan*), in the middle of the garden. When God speaks to Moses for the first time, it is מִתּוֹךְ הַסְּנֶה (*mi-tokh ha-seneh*), from within the Burning Bush. Subtly, God commands the Israelites to build a sanctuary so that He may dwell, not in *it*, but בְּתוֹכָם (*be-tokham*), in their midst.

Heroic Samson destroys the Philistines, bringing down the house by taking hold of עַמּוּדֵי הַתָּוֶךְ (*ammudei ha-tavekh*), the central pillars. And let us not forget David's famous lament for Jonathan and Saul, "[How the mighty are fallen] בְּתוֹךְ הַמִּלְחָמָה (*be-tokh ha-milhama*), in the midst of the battle."

Several charming rabbinic anecdotes use our root. Rabban Gamaliel announces that any applicant to his academy who is not תּוֹכוֹ כְּבָרוֹ (*tokho ke-varo*), the same inside as outside—totally genuine, without duplicity—will be rejected. When Elisha Ben Avuyah becomes an apostate, his disciple Rabbi Meir refuses to abandon him; the Talmud declares metaphorically that Meir found a pomegranate, discarded the unsavory rind and תּוֹכוֹ אָכַל (*tokho akhal*), ate the fruit within. The rabbis are so confident of humanity's essential goodness that they maintain מִתּוֹךְ שֶׁלֹּא בָּא לִשְׁמָה לִשְׁמָה (*mi-*

tokh she-lo lishma ba lishma), a mitzva done initially from self-interest will eventually be done for its own sake.

Today, to settle a dispute one calls in a מְתַוֵּךְ (*me-tavvekh*), mediator. If we're lucky, he will arrange a compromise תּוֹךְ שָׁבוּעַ (*tokh shavu'a*), within a week. Sometimes one resolves an issue תּוֹךְ כְּדֵי דִבּוּר (*tokh kedei dibbur*), in the middle of speaking, that is, in a flash. Anyone who has studied at a בֵּית סֵפֶר תִּיכוֹן (*beit sefer tikhon*), high school—originally "middle" school—knows that Israel is located בְּתוֹךְ (*be-tokh*), within, the region of הַיָּם הַתִּיכוֹן (*ha-yam ha-tikhon*), the Mediterranean Sea, which used to be the central sea.

Of course, even an outsider knows this. What an insider understands בְּתוֹךְ תּוֹכוֹ (*be-tokh tokho*), in his innermost being, is that all these Hebrew treasures derive from a single root.

108

Turn It and Turn It

ת-ו-ר

tav-vav-resh

Accord ing to humorist Ephraim Kishon, when Israelis are asked לַעֲמוֹד בַּתּוֹר (*la-amod ba-tor*), to stand in line, there are always a "privileged few" who consider themselves exceptions to the rule. Since everybody in Israel is a somebody, observes Kishon, nobody patiently waits his turn. The root ת-ו-ר (*tav, vav, resh*), from which we get turn—in addition to many other seemingly unconnected derivations—is similarly exceptional among Hebrew roots.

Scripture uses our root to narrate critical moments in Jewish history, as when Moses sends 12 men לָתוּר (*la-tur*), to explore, or spy out, the Land of Canaan, or when תֹּר אֶסְתֵּר (*tor ester*), Esther's turn, comes to spend a night with the king. Biblical merchants who roam the land, אַנְשֵׁי הַתָּרִים (*anshei ha-tarim*), prefigure today's traveling salesmen. When God informs King David that not he, but his son Solomon will build the Temple, David accepts this as a promise that his dynasty will endure forever. He sees this future—in the Anchor Bible translation—in the expression תּוֹרַת הָאָדָם (*torat ha-adam*), "the generation to come."

Numbers enjoins the Hebrews, לֹא תָתוּרוּ אַחֲרֵי לְבַבְכֶם (*lo taturu aharei levavkhem*), "Do not go about after your heart's desire," and Ecclesiastes confesses self-indulgence, saying תַּרְתִּי בְּלִבִּי (*tarti be-libbi*), "I followed my heart." The lover in Song of Songs offers his beloved תּוֹרֵי זָהָב (*torei zahav*), stringed necklaces of gold—not to be confused with תּוֹר הַזָּהָב (*tor ha-zahav*), the Golden Age, the era of extraordinary Jewish creativity in Muslim Spain. In a more gloomy context, the title of Aharon Appelfeld's 1978 novel, תּוֹר הַפְּלָאוֹת (*tor ha-pela'ot*), *The Age of Wonders*, can refer to the catastrophic historical "era" in which the novel is set or the perplexing adolescent "age" of its main protagonist.

Eliezer Ben-Yehuda records in his modern Hebrew dictionary a belief among certain Hasidic circles that after a righteous man dies, he is brought before an angel tasked לְתַיְּרוֹ (*le-tairo*), to guide him, into God's presence. Today, guides can be found at Israel's מִשְׂרָד הַתַּיָּרוּת (*misrad ha-tayyarut*), Tourism Ministry. At the theater, applaud the actor who performs the תּוֹר (*tor*), role, of the play's hero. To fill a prescription after hours, find a בֵּית מֶרְקַחַת תּוֹרָן (*beit merkahat toran*), on-duty pharmacy. Admire the concept of תּוֹרָנוּת (*toranut*), service by rotation, by visiting a kibbutz and observing תּוֹרָנוּת הַמִּטְבָּח (*toranut ha-mitbah*), shared KP duty.

If you call ahead לִקְבֹּעַ תּוֹר (*likbo'a tor*), to make an appointment, you won't have to rush to the front of the line when the clerk calls out הַבָּא בַּתּוֹר (*ha-ba ba-tor*), "Next!"

109

Luscious to the Core

ת-פ-ח
tav-feh-het

In spring, a young man's fancy turns to love. And in autumn? That's when all thoughts turn to—apples. In addition to American apple pie, in the fall many Jewish families dish up תַּפּוּחַ בִּדְבַשׁ (*tappu'ah bi-devash*), apple dipped in honey, to usher in a sweet new year.

To wonder about the Hebrew source of the apple is to raise a question with a long-winded answer. Despite popular assumptions, there is no תַּפּוּחַ (*tappu'ah*), apple, in the biblical story of the Garden of Eden. Scriptural apples fuse with springtime love in the Song of Songs, where the lover is כְּתַפּוּחַ בַּעֲצֵי הַיַּעַר (*ke-tappu'ah ba-atsei ha-ya'ar*), "like an apple tree among the forest's trees." Commenting on this verse, the Talmud (Shabbat 88a) asks, how is the Jewish people like an apple tree? Just as an apple tree first produces its fruit and then its leaves, so too the Israelites at Sinai agreed to observe the mitzvot and then to hear what they were.

In Hebrew, it appears, apples come from two roots—ת-פ-ח (*tav, feh, het*) and נ-פ-ח (*nun, feh, het*)—both of which have to do with breathing, swelling, puffing up. Some scholars trace the word's source to the fact that the apple "breathes" a pleasant aroma into the air. For others, its puffed-up shape leads to its name. Neither of these conjectures is מְנוּפָּח (*menuppah*), overblown.

Interestingly, a *tappu'ah* is not always an apple, as in תַּפּוּחַ עָקֵב (*tappu'ah akev*), the fleshy part of the heel. In the Temple, the word *tappu'ah* was used for that part of the altar where the ashes were placed in a pile. And an ill person can be תָּפוּחַ רָעָב (*tafu'ah ra'av*), bloated from starvation.

In modern Hebrew, the תַּפּוּחַ אָדָם הָרִאשׁוֹן (*tappu'ah adam ha-rishon*), Adam's apple, is also not a real apple. Nor is a תַּפּוּחַ אֲדָמָה (*tappu'ah adama*), potato (cf. *pomme de terre*), or a תַּפּוּחַ זָהָב

(*tappu'ah zahav*), orange—more commonly known by the abbreviated תַּפּוּז (*tappuz*). The rabbis observe that a תָּפֵחַ (*tefah*), swollen fruit, may shrivel, but that the opposite does not occur.

In the kitchen, one can speak of תְּפִיחָה (*tefiha*), the rising of dough, or תַּפִּיחִית (*tappihit*), a puffy soufflé. And then there is תְּפִיחוּת (*tefihut*), the swelling caused by a wound.

Words that come from the *nun-feh-het* root include נַפָּח (*nappah*), a blacksmith, who uses bellows; סִיר נָפוּחַ (*sir nafu'ah*), a boiling pot (look at the bubbles); מַפּוּחִית (*mappuhit*), harmonica; and נַפַּחַת (*nappahat*), emphysema.

If these derivations leave you breathless, you might wish to quote the Song of Songs yourself, saying, רַפְּדוּנִי בַּתַּפּוּחִים (*rappduni ba-tappuhim*), "Refresh me with apples." Make mine strudel.

110

Tikkun My Fancy

ת-ק-נ

tav-kof-nun

The Jewish boulevardier, strolling along Second Avenue during Yiddish theater's heyday, sees a poster for King Lear—*fartaytcht un farbesert*, translated and improved. "Not surprising," he murmurs. After all, improving Shakespeare is straightforward compared to תִּקּוּן עוֹלָם (*tikkun olam*), the millennial mission of the Jews to repair the entire world. *Tikkun olam* comes from ת-ק-נ (*tav, kof, nun*), to put in order, a root that also gives us another buzzword, תְּקִינוּת פּוֹלִיטִית (*tekinut politit*), political correctness.

The root appears several times in Scripture, with different meanings. Ecclesiastes tells us that King Solomon תִּקֵּן מְשָׁלִים הַרְבֵּה (*tiken meshalim harbeh*), tested the soundness of many maxims, such as מִי יוּכַל לְתַקֵּן (*mi yukhal le-takken*), who can straighten (what God has twisted)?

The rabbis use our root to describe an action to benefit society. In the Shabbat morning "*El Adon*" hymn, we are told that God הִתְקִין צוּרַת הַלְּבָנָה (*hitkin tsurat ha-levanah*), arranged the phases of the moon for man's sake. *Pirke Avot* teaches metaphorically that before you enter the ballroom, i.e., the next world, הֶתְקֵן עַצְמְךָ (*hetken atsmekha*), straighten your clothes in the vestibule. A תִּקּוּן (*tikkun*) is, among other arrangements, a book arranged to teach the musical notes of the Torah reading.

And then there are the famous תַּקָּנוֹת (*takkanot*), reforms, promulgated by the rabbis, the most dramatic of which was that of Rabbeinu Gershom (965–1028), prohibiting polygamy. In Modern Hebrew there are civil uses for the word, as in תַּקָּנוֹת לִשְׁעַת חֵרוּם (*takkanot li-she'at herum*), emergency measures.

Today, an editor might tell the printer תַּקֵּן הָרֶוַח (*taken ha-revah*), align the spaces between words correctly. Or the מְכוֹן הַתְּקָנִים

(*mekhon ha-tekanim*), standards institute, might suggest prohibiting the import of goods that don't meet its תֶּקֶן (*teken*), standard. The principal, to determine class size, will refer bureaucratically to the תֶּקֶן (*teken*), set of school regulations. Sometimes one doesn't get a job because there was no תֶּקֶן (*teken*), slot, for it in the budget.

An adjective derived from our root, תִּקְנִי (*tikni*), is found in זְמַן תִּקְנִי (*zeman tikni*), standard time, and לָשׁוֹן תִּקְנִית (*lashon tiknit*), standard language. Then there is תָּקִין (*takin*), normal, regular, in good working order. Many Israelis express the desire for חַיִּים תְּקִינִים (*hayyim tekinim*), a normal life. To do that it is often necessary to live according to a תַּקָּנוֹן (*takkanon*), code of conduct.

That doesn't mean you can't take some liberties, especially if your goal is to improve Shakespeare—or the world.

About the Author

D r. Joseph Lowin was most recently Director of the National Center for the Hebrew Language (NCHL) in New York City. Previously, Lowin was Director of Cultural Services at the National Foundation for Jewish Culture, Director of the Midrasha Institute of Jewish Studies, and National Director of Jewish Education at Hadassah. Having earned his Ph.D. from Yale University, Lowin has held faculty appointments at Yale, the University of Miami, and Touro College. Lowin has been a Fulbright Fellow at the Sorbonne in Paris and a Jerusalem Fellow at the Hebrew University in Israel.

While there, he had a weekly radio segment on Israel's national radio station, Kol Yisrael. The segment, called "Hebrew Roots and Sources," reached listeners globally. Lowin's columns on the Hebrew language have appeared in Hadassah Magazine for more than 30 years and he has adapted 200 of these columns into the books *HebrewSpeak* (1995) and *HebrewTalk* (2004). *Hebrew Matters* is the third volume in the series. Lowin's book, *Cyntha Ozick,* on the literary universe of Cynthia Ozick, appeared in Twayne's United States Authors Series in 1988. In addition to his 300 essays on Hebrew etymology, Lowin has published more than 140 essays and reviews dealing with Jewish literature. In 2017, Lexington Books published *Art and the Artist in the Contemporary Israeli Novel,* Lowin's book on the conjunction of literary art and the Jewish textual tradition. Lowin currently lives in New York City.

Suggestions for Further Hebrew Browsing

Reuven Alkalai. *The Complete English-Hebrew Dictionary.* **Lambda Publishers, 2012.**
This is the standard Hebrew-English dictionary used by scholars and students. It is accepted by all as highly authoritative.

Abraham Solomonick. *Maskilon I, II, III.* **Jerusalem: Gefen Publishing House, 2001.**
This three-volume set puts together a *Hebrew-English Dictionary of Verb-Roots*; a *Practical Hebrew Grammar for English Speakers*; and a *Hebrew-English Learner's Dictionary.* This is a rich reference tool in a small format. If you can find, or afford, only the first volume, it's still worth it. (For the record, somewhere in real space there is a fourth volume that provides this information in Russian.)

Ernest Klein. *Comprehensive Etymological Dictionary of the Hebrew Language for Readers of English.* **New York: Macmillan, 1987.**
If you are a true lover of Hebrew etymology, one who likes to browse aimlessly through the pages of a dictionary, looking for whatever may pop up to excite your fancy, you should do your best to get your hands on this precious volume. It delivers even more than what its title promises.

Yaacov Choueka. *Young Rav Milim.* **Steimatzky/C.E.T./Yediot Ahronot/Sifrei Hemed, 1996**
Those willing to challenge themselves and let their reach modestly exceed their grasp with a Hebrew-Hebrew Dictionary will find themselves duly rewarded. This is a delightful two-volume dictionary with lots of illustrations, cultural sidebars, and other

guardrails designed for Israeli students and pupils. It teaches English speakers almost as much about life in Israel as it does about the Hebrew language. And it provides easy access. As such, it should be on the shelves of any English-speaking household that has middle-school, high-school, university or life-long-learning students of Hebrew language and culture in its ranks.

Joseph Lowin. *HebrewSpeak: An Insider's Guide to the Way Jews Think.* **Rowman & Littlefield Publishers, 1995.**

Joseph Lowin. *HebrewTalk: 101 Hebrew Roots and the Stories They Tell.* **EKS Publishers, 2004.**

Jeremy Bernstein. *Hebrew Roots, Jewish Routes: A Tribal Language in a Global World.* **Berhrman House Publishers, 2019.**

<u>**Online Apps**</u>:
Since some of the books above may be out of print and therefore hard to find except in academic libraries or specialized bookstores, we suggest a few handy sites online.

From The Rusty Brick, a developer of Jewish Apps. Their *English/Hebrew Translator* is the ideal source for someone who needs a quick look-up of a word or phrase. It provides a neat, no-clutter simple translation of words in both directions, Hebrew/English, English/Hebrew. Be careful, however. It provides only one option, where there may be as many as twenty others lying somewhere in the background. For those who can stand slightly more clutter, go to Google Translate.

Balashon – Hebrew Language Detective investigates all areas of Hebrew, including slang; related languages like Aramaic, Arabic, Akkadian and Yiddish; how foreign languages like Greek, Latin and English have entered Hebrew; and how Hebrew has affected those languages as well. Discusses the meanings of words, with a focus on etymology. For those who can handle a busy blog.

From Sefaria: Torah, Talmud, & More. Clicking on one Hebrew word will open you up to a world of Hebraica and Judaica. This creatively designed app can be searched by word or phrase as it explores thousands of Jewish texts that can be read both in Hebrew and English translation. Its development is ongoing but what it has accomplished thus far is awe-inspiring.

Akademia for You: The Israel Hebrew Language Academy e-Newsletter in English. https://en.hebrew-academy.org.il/join-us/join-our-mailing-list/

This is the newest thing, online, for English-speaking learners of Hebrew and for Hebrew teachers as well. And, it comes from Israel's Hebrew Language Academy. Accessible to a readership with a range of Hebrew levels, this pithy publication provides illuminating content capable of enriching not only beginners and intermediate students of Hebrew but also informing even advanced speakers with a strong background in Jewish texts. For now, it comes out a few times a year and consists of several bite-size articles, often with links to further reading (usually in Hebrew) on the Academy's website. Recurring columns examine holiday-related material; names; idioms and expressions; and relevant terms.

www.ingramcontent.com/pod-product-compliance
Lightning Source LLC
Chambersburg PA
CBHW060914120626
46553CB00001B/316